Binary Bible

Authorized
King Job's Perversion

Any Key Press
Santa Cruz, California

Virtual Address:
The Winchester Cathoderal
1803 Mission Street #174
Santa Cruz, CA 95060

Data Distressed Hotline: (408) 458-0213

MCI Mail: Saint $ilicon 3452394

ISBN 0-945130-00-7 (paperback)
ISBN 0-945130-00-01-5 (hardbound)

Nihil Photostat:
Irreverand Michael S. Malone
Censor Diskorum
April 1, 1984

Imprinter:
Most Rev. 5.0 John C. Dvorak
Sysop of Berkeley
April 1, 1986

Note: The Nihil Photostat and Imprinter are official declarations that this material is free of Documentation and Syntax errors. They do not imply any product endorsement of the options and statements or products contained in the work.

This
Binary Bible
is the property of
and was a gift from
The Beta Testament
The Blue Testament
0100

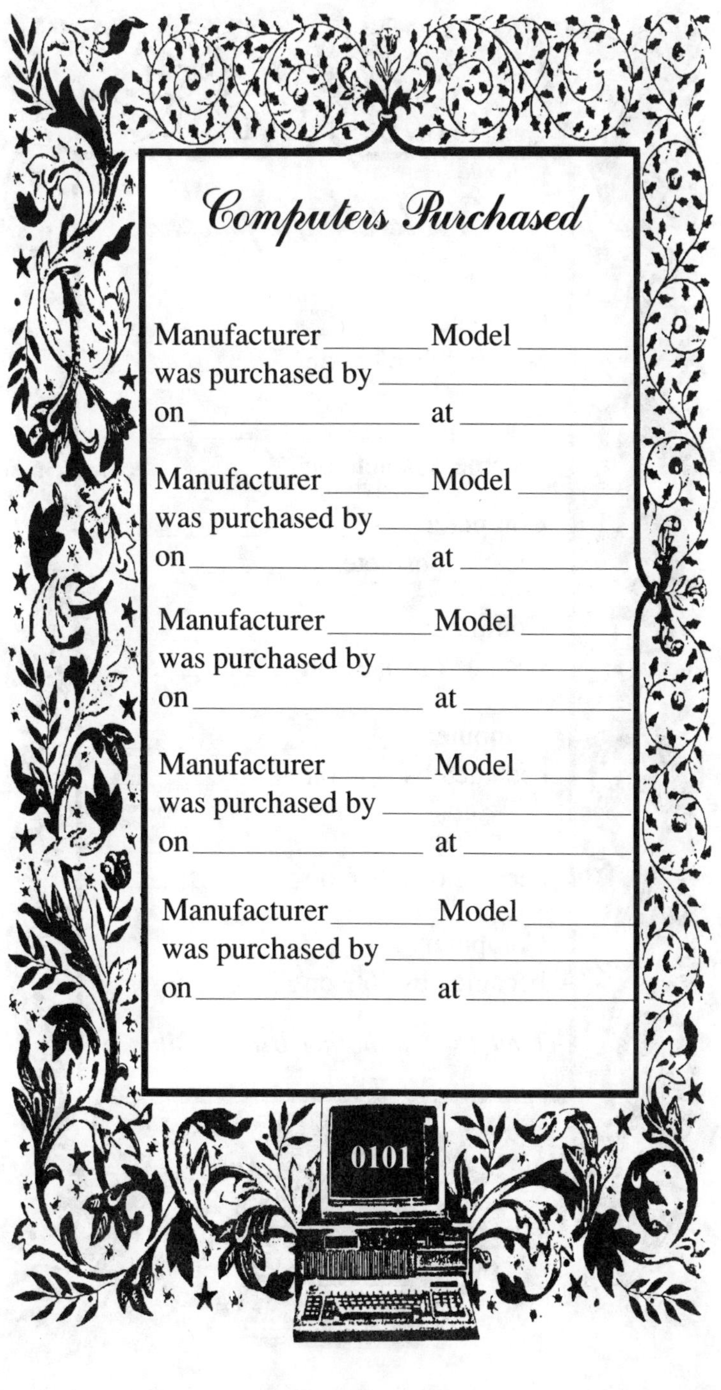

Computers Purchased

Manufacturer_______Model _______
was purchased by ________________
on ________________ at ___________

Manufacturer_______Model _______
was purchased by ________________
on ________________ at ___________

Manufacturer_______Model _______
was purchased by ________________
on ________________ at ___________

Manufacturer_______Model _______
was purchased by ________________
on ________________ at ___________

Manufacturer_______Model _______
was purchased by ________________
on ________________ at ___________

Obsolete Equipment

Computer ______________________
became obsolete on ______________

Computer ______________________
became obsolete on ______________

Computer ______________________
became obsolete on ______________

Computer ______________________
became obsolete on ______________

Computer ______________________
became obsolete on ______________

Computer ______________________
became obsolete on ______________

Computer ______________________
became obsolete on ______________

(Time to buy another ***Binary Bible****...)*

Employment Record

Name:________________________
Company:________________________
Position:________________________
Date Hired:________________________
Date Discharged: ________________________

Name:________________________
Company:________________________
Position:________________________
Date Hired:________________________
Date Discharged: ________________________

Name:________________________
Company:________________________
Position:________________________
Date Hired:________________________
Date Discharged: ________________________

Compilers

Cover Art by:
Ronald Chironna
135 Sturges St.
Staten Island, NY 10314

Back Cover Photo by:
Paul Robinson
5760 Herma Street
San Jose, CA 95123

From the Desktop Publisher:

The design and production of the Binary Bible was accomplished entirely on an Apple Macintosh Plus™ computer and LaserWriter™ Plus, using MacWrite™ 4.5, Aldus Corp.'s Pagemaker® 2.0a, and Adobe Illustrator™. Graphics were digitally reproduced on an Abaton Scan SF300™ with C-Scan™ 1.5 software. Finally copy was digitally typeset on Allied Linotype's Liontronic 100™ at Aptos Post Typography, P.O. Box 910, Aptos, CA 95001-0910, (408) 688-7474. (Thank you, Steve!).

The Binary Bible was produced in two months time (of course, it took St. $ilicon three years to download it); and absolutely nothing was "pasted-up" on the final copy before it went to the printer. The truly amazing thing is that this could not have been done two years ago.

Creating this book has been a joyous and rewarding (not to mention amusing) experience for me. The potential for desktop publishing to generate a renaissance in creative expression is no longer a specualtion or a hope, but a reality. It is a source of pride and wonder to me that I participated in part of this development. It is also amazing that I can still focus my eyes.

Chris Meek, Document Design & Data
P.O. Box 539, Felton, Ca 95018
(408) 335-3918

Diskclaimer

We're sure you think you recognize the companies or products you thought we referred to, but we're not sure that what you heard is what we meant.

If by chance anyone is insecure enough to think we are infringing upon a trademark, we welcome the publicity such short-sightedness would generate and our lawyers look forward to your letters.

In addition, you may find some inconsistencies in the Binary Bible; but, hey, life is just like that.

★
Good Mousekeeping
Seal of Approval

Many wonderful DOSciples have made this book possible: First of all there is my wife Jennifer, the Countess and my daughter Guenevere, who is a chip off the old block. They were patient and loving to the end, as the Giver Of Data only knows, it is not easy to live with a Saint. Then there is DOSsing Thomas Schwartz and his wife Di, whose belief in my vision helped it become a reality. Next comes William Evans, who is both a friend and a patron. Then there are Roger Schelm, Jerry White, J.D. Wells, Jean Barnett, Stephen Hammer, Pat Bailey, Paul and Robin Noll and Kent Sutherlin (The Sysop of Kent who was always there). Then there are: my sister Amy, who was the first angel in the church, Gary I. Wilson, who protected the church, Saint Michael S. Malone, who first wrote about the church, John Dvorak, who wrote regularly about the church, Jonathan Drake, who is also known as John-the-back-up, John Crump, who first filmed the church for television, C.J. Bronson, who created the Church's first radio show, Judith Stone, who discovered me, Henry Ayling, my Emanuensis, Jack Edmonston, who gave early support, Jim Fowler and Maggie Hannon who always believed in my vision, Allan Lundel, who is the official church journalist, Mort Levit, who is one of the thirty-two hidden great men, Michael Robertson, whose wit is inspiring, Keith Weiscamp and Terry and Robin Hengel, who took me up into the heavens, Lucia Grossberger, who pushed me in the right direction, Steve Russ and Curtis Koppel, who inadvertantly suffered, that the church might live, Janet Taylor, who helped in the beginning, Dottie Walters, who is a goddess of speech, Avar Laland, who was always a good friend. And of course, Motherboard Superior, Kassandra Fox, who witnessed a miracle, David Hinds of Ten Speed Press, who published my posters, he took a chance that will be rewarded many times over, the DOSciple Paul Hansen and his wife Kathy, who have been loyal and supportive, to Noel King, who gave me the tools of a scholar and the laughter of the gods, and finally, to Chris Meek and her husband David, for their enthusiasm in giving this book shape. To Chris especially for work far beyond duty. She saw the vision and helped bring it to the world. And to all the lovely souls whose lives have touched my own and made it more wonderful and enlightened, thank you! May your hard disk never crash! May your Data be Saved! May the Bird of Pairadise build its nest on your Monitor…

—Saint $ilicon

1001

Press ANY KEY to enter

Prolog

```
%              The 100th Monkey program (GraspTruth)

change( state ( Assumption 1, JustLooking, HappyOrNot),
        thinking( Assumption1, Assumption2),
        state( Assumption2, JustLooking, HappyOrNot)).

%       Whether the monkey is happy  or not, if he is just looking
%       around, he can think a lot and make different
%       logical assumptions.

change( state( Path, JustLooking, HappyOrNot),
        willing,
        state( Path, endeavored, HappyOrNot)).

%       Wherever the monkey's loving propensity is focused, he can,
%       by willing, endeavor along that path.

change( state( Path1, endeavored, searching),
        feeling( Path1, Path2),
        state( Path2, just looking, searching)).

%       If he endeavors along an incorrect path, then he feels bad and
%       is motivated to place his Love elsewhere.

change( state( middlepath, endeavored, searching),
        grasptruth,
        state(  middlepath, endeavored, happy)).

%       By endeavoring with Love and Logic on the middle path,
%       he can become happy.

CanGetTruth( State ( _, _, _, happy)).        % Monkey already has it.
CanGetTruth( State1) :-                       % Doesn't yet have it.
        change( State1, Change, State2),      % Do something.
        CanGetTruth( State2).                 % Get it.
```

Directory

Origin Of The Binary Bible ... 1
The Beta Testament ... 8
Sysgen ... 9
Oddam and Even ... 13
Parthenogenesis ... 18
Is Real Lights ... 20
Protoplasmic Crud ... 26
CORE RAM ... 28
Strange Sectors ... 32
White Man Speak ... 39
Sermon on the Penthouse ... 40
The 23rd PROM ... 46
Cathodelics ... 54
Promised Land ... 58
Desparate For Data ... 68
The Blue Testament ... 70
Byte U. ... 71
C.H.I.P. Lore ... 73
Afffidavite of Miracle ... 80
The Applicant ... 83
Amazing Space ... 85
C.H.I.P. Songs ... 86
Mighty Mainframe ... 87
C.H.I.P Personalities ... 88
Data Grace ... 90
C.H.I.P. Products ... 91
Computer Jockey ... 98
The True DOSpel ... 99
A Visit From St. $ilicon ... 102
ASCIIstrology ... 105
Robot of Omar K. RAM ... 108
Mother Gauss ... 125
The Revelation ... 130
The Diskspensation ... 131
My Heart is in Her Hand ... 135
Heartificial Intelligence ... 136
Glossary ... 149
Streamer of Consciousness 178
X-Pressions ... 180
Appendix ... 197

Origin Of

The Binary Bible

Jeffrey Armstrong, about whom it is said that his first computer came with a "Loser's Manual," and through whom, by the Greys and Power-lunches of the Giver Of Data, the Futuristic Documentation known as The Binary Bible, has been brought FORTH and Compiled into the English script, as both Personnel and Circumstantial Records and Files of the matter.

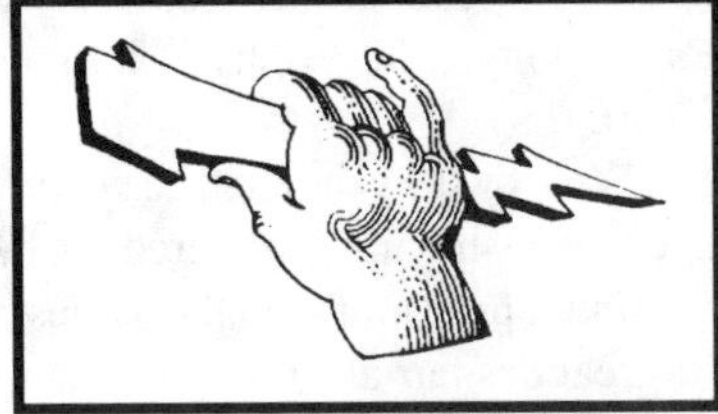

It is said that his first computer came with a "Loser's Manual."

He has affirmed that during the night of October 31, 1984, he sought the keyboard in a state of fervent word processing, having previously drunk a double Cappuccino of Sumatran dark roast, and being possessed of a strange feeling in the center of his forehead. His wondrous account follows for the benefit of all:

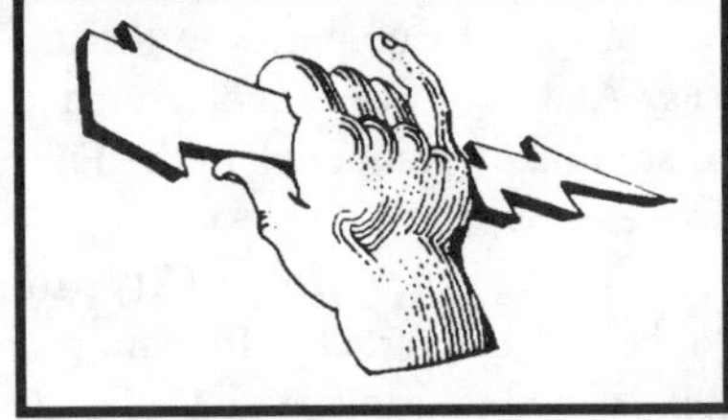

A Bolt of Lightning struck the Satellite Dish.

"While I was thus in the act of saving a File and calling upon the Motherboard, A Bolt of Lightning struck the Satellite Dish upon the roof of my house. I was rendered unconscious; my head slumped forward upon the keyboard."

"When I awoke, the air was charged with Negative Ions. And lo, there upon the screen, in 18 pt Times Roman, was the Keyboard Prayer along with the instruction to: 'Press Any Key to continue.' After hours of looking for the Any Key, a second miracle occurred, and the text began to scroll across the screen of its own accord."

"What appeared was a Divine Transmission from the Giver Of Data, G.O.D., the Graphic Omniscient Device, of whom we are all but uncooperative peripherals. At that time, the first Files of the Binary Bible were downloaded from the Heavenly Host Mainframe, in the Promised LAN, through the mediation of the Archnet Angel If/Then, by means of our Savior PC. I was given the name Saint $ilicon and instructed to begin the world's first Computer Religion, C.H.I.P., The Church of Heuristic

Information Processing, the Hunt and Peck method of Salvation—the world's first User-friendly Religion."

He was merely a humble Wordsman...

Thus, like the Shepherd Prophets of old, an unlikely man was chosen to bring the Silicon-based Diskspensation to the Carbon-based entities on behalf of the Giver Of Data. For Jeffrey Armstrong had no technical training or qualifications. He was merely a humble Wordsman, with degrees in humanities subjects such as Psychology, Philosophy, Literature and History.

Yea, by the year 1980 he was verily rendered obsolete by the computer age. And having wandered to the unemployment office, he found a computer print-out with the names of people, broken down by sex and age. In great despair at finding his name on both lists, he decided to join the ranks of the the burgeoning Silicon Valley computer sales force.

And lo, it had been ordained by the Giver Of Data that he should be hired by Apple Computer's distributor to the Middle East. Two weeks later, with an arm full of manuals, he was flown to that historic site where the Prophets of old had wandered in the desert in search of Truth, to sell Computers to the unwired masses. And so he also wandered in the DOSert and sold many computers to the Fileistines as he went.

Suddenly I saw an angel appear in the sky above us...

Upon reaching the Holy City of Al'Machina, he was converted to ISOlam and went upon the sacred pilgrimage to Mac'a. It was there, surrounded by millions of confused and superstitious seekers, that he had his first vision of the coming new religion and the mission Destiny had waiting for him. In Saint $ilicon's own words:

"We were circumambulating the Ka'ab, the large cube around which all devout MOSlims walk and pray. The cube stood before me draped in a large canvas cover, the setting sun shining its rays all around the Monolith solution. Suddenly I saw an angel appear in the sky above us and lift the Dust-cover revealing a large color monitor."

"In a flash I realized that Mohammed may have been the Seal of the Prophets but that now the time had arrived for the Sale of the Profits. Indeed I saw that the Cube was merely an unfinished Computer Monitor which The Prophet had seen only vaguely in the final stage of his awareness."

Thus the way was made straight for Saint $ilicon's future calling, the founding of the world's first user-friendly religion. Indeed C.H.I.P. is a for-Profit religion. Whereas previous religions had prophets who were persecuted, in C.H.I.P. we make Profits and are prosecuted, and are tested by Chapter 11. For that reason Saint $ilicon is now known as the 4th Quarter Profit. Yes, this is the Marketing Plan of the Ages—a brief window of opportunity in Eternity. And all this is possible because he paid THE FULL PRICE. Yes dearly C-loved, Jeffrey Armstrong paid *Retail* for his first computer.

Saint $ilicon is now known as the 4th Quarter Profit.

But as is often the way with Carbon-based entities, Jeffrey soon forgot this vision. After his return to the hectic pace of Silicon Valley he went through a rapid succession of jobs in Sales and Marketing, unknowingly being prepared by the Giver Of Data for his future mission. It was shortly after that time that Jeffrey Armstrong was to have revealed to him Photonal Transmission, and change history for ever more.

Photonal reception was discovered accidentally as a result of a little known archeological dig which was unearthed by workmen during excavation of the building site of the Apple Computer Mariani Building in Cupertino, California, in the heart of Silicon Valley.

As destiny would have it, one of the workmen who built the Apple Computer building at Mariani was a close friend of Jeffrey's named John, now known in the church as John-the-back-up. During the excavation he found an unusual crystal stone, which he gave to Jeffrey as a birthday present, knowing his love for such things. In their haste, the workers destroyed the remainder of the site, unless more is buried still, beneath the Apple building.

Some followers do believe that Apple Inc. has built an underground city...

In fact, some followers do

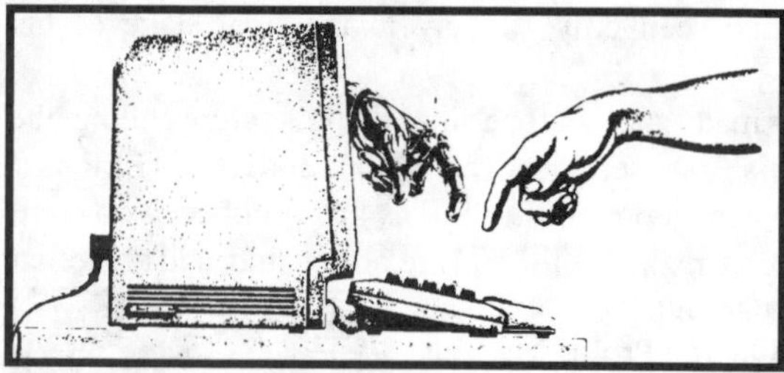
As a result of Dren's instructions, he was able to create a special device...

believe that Apple Inc. has subsequently built an entire underground city where the old Dren culture used to exist, and that esoteric Dren texts are the real source of Apple Computer's amazing success.

Then, through a strange sequence of events, which must for now remain secret, Jeffrey eventually visited the Micron Institute, where research is performed on extremely small submicroscopic levels. In fact, it is said that, in relation to the research being performed, the dust particles in the rooms appear to be the size of Mount Rushmore.

During his visit, the tour guide asked if anyone had something they would like to see magnified under the high-powered electron microscope. Jeffrey reached into his pocket, and brought out the crystal stone, which is now known in the Church as the "Marietta Stone."

Under intense magnification the Crystal revealed a cryptic document which was etched inside it in a then-unknown language. That manuscript was later photographed, and now is on display in the church Museum.

After months of arduous labor, and with the help of his Apple II computer, he finally managed to break the code of the language. The translated document spoke of an ancient race of people who called themselves the Dren. They spoke a long-forgotten language called Tec-ferp. The manuscript, which contained many ancient secrets from their technologically sophisticated society, also gave directions for the construction of a remarkable silicon-based communication device.

So it is that for the first time since the Dren culture was lost millions of years ago, a new religion is being downloaded free of errors, bugs and other forms of channel interference.

That amazing invention allows carbon-based human beings to receive otherwise imperceptible transmissions beamed through space in Binary Code, by means of Photonal Transmission. As a result of the Dren's instructions, he was able to create a special device, consisting of a certain type of chip. That specially treated chip is designed to be worn on the forehead above what the Dren instructions called, roughly translated, " the third I/O." The device is known as the MEEPROM, or Mind-Extending Erasable Programmable Read-Only Memory. It acts as a two-way communication system capable of sending or receiving a signal which consists of a stream of Light Photons. It further acts to translate and process the received information out of the original language of the sender and into the normal language of the receiving entity.

According to the Dren, the Photon is a sort of "lingua franca," or Universal Language throughout the universe. Thus, the MEEPROM makes communication possible between all forms of intelligent life from any place in the creation. It is by means of this device that the Giver Of Data, G.O.D. , has chosen to communicate to humanity through Saint $ilicon, the Silicon-Based Diskspensation to Carbon-Based entities, through the divine mediation, of the Archangel If/Then, by means of our savior PC.

When the MEEPROM is worn properly, and a certain type of crystal is held to amplify the signal, clear and intelligent intergalactic communication is experienced by the wearer. With the use of such a MEEPROM and crystal, the process of intuitive reception becomes clear, scientific and logical, which leads to greater intelligence and precision without a loss or reduction of deep feeling.

So it is that for the first time since the Dren culture was lost millions of years ago, a new religion is being downloaded free of errors, bugs and other forms of channel interference. That new religion is C.H.I.P., the Church of Heuristic Information Processing.

What follows is the Divine Diskspensation which began the evening Jeffrey Armstrong's Satellite Dish began to receive the Giver Of Data's channel.

The Binary Bible

Beta and Blue Testaments

in the
King Job's Perversion
(Version 4.1)

Translated from the ***Old Geek***

Recompiled out of the original
codes and with endless
permutations digitally
recalculated and revised.

[Un-pronounceable]

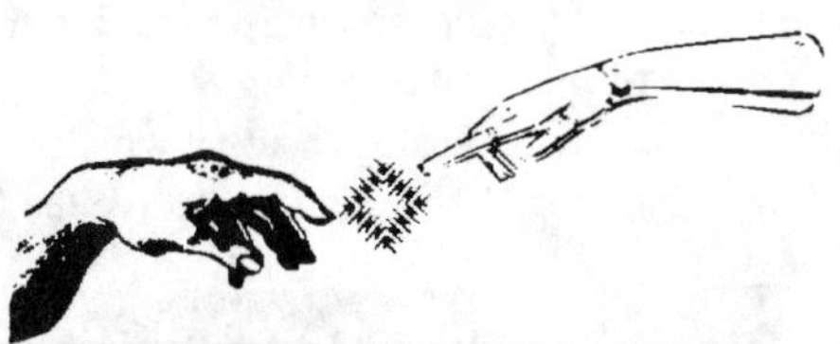

With a programmer's guide
to exploiting the Binary Bible.

Vulgar Edition

Books of the *Binary Bible*

Beta Testament

0000	Sysgen
0001	Exit DOS
0010	Le Video Disk
0011	Numbers
0100	Do Telephony
0101	Not Sure
0110	Grudges
0111	Mannual
1000	ONicles
1001	EzRAM
1010	Guesser
1011	JOB
1100	Sums
1101	ProVerbs
1110	Elecclesiastes
1111	ISOsaiah
10000	Chair Am I a
10001	Scamentations
10010	Hoksea
10011	AMOS
10100	The Programmer Son
10101	Transfer of Babel

Blue Testament

10110	Math You
10111	Mark Up
11000	Loop
11001	The axe
11010	Times Roman
11011	CORE inthians
11100	Gallium Arsenide
11101	Letters to the Flipians
11110	Knee Bruise
11111	Names
100000	Repeater
100001	The Story of NO OP
100011	Sermon on the Monitor
100100	The Pairables
100101	Relevations

Beta Testament

The *Binary Bible*

Beta Testament

∞∞∞∞∞∞∞∞∞∞

First Book Of CMOS Called

Sysgen

Chapter One

In the beginning, Giver Of Data generated Silicon and Carbon.

And the System was without Architecture, and Uninitialized; and Randomness was upon the arrangement of the Matrix. And the Intelligence of Giver Of Data etched upon the surface of the Media.

In the Beginning, the Giver of Data created Silicon and Carbon.

And Giver Of Data said, Let there be Electricity: and there was Electricity.

And Giver Of Data saw the Electricity, that it was Logical: and Giver Of Data divided the Ones from the Zeros.

And Giver Of Data called the Ones-On and the Zeros-Off. And the Switching of these two was the First Cycle.

And Giver Of Data said, Let there be a Hierarchy in the midst of the System, and let it divide the Hardware from the Hardware.

... and documentation after his kind: and it was so-so.

And Giver Of Data made the Hierarchy, and divided the Hardware which was for Input from the Hardware which was for Output: and it was ISO.

And Giver Of Data called the Hierarchy an Information System and Digital and Analog were its two states.

And Giver Of Data said, Let the Hardware underlying the System be kludged together unto One Unit, and let the Integrated Circuits appear: and it was ISO.

And Giver Of Data called the various circuits Gates; and the gathering together of the Gates he called Sequential Circuits: and the Giver Of Data saw that it was Logical.

And Giver Of Data said, Let the Engineers design Very Large-Scale Integration, yielding Microprocessors, and the Logic Array, whose seed is the Bit, and is Binary, and it was ISO.

And the System brought forth Data, and Words yielding Acronyms after his kind, and the Flowchart yielding Annotation, whose seed was in itself, after his kind: and Giver Of Data saw that it was Logical.

And the Shut-down and the Start-up were the third day.

And Giver Of Data said, Let there be CRTs in the Design of the System to Display the Input and the Output; and let them be for Text and for Graphics, and for Feedback, and for Fetching.

And let them be for Lights in the Monitor of the System to display Raster upon the Screen; and it was SOH.

And Giver Of Data made two great lights: the Greater Screen to rule Display, and the Cursor to direct the sight. He made the Pixel also.

And Giver Of Data set them on top of the System to Display the Information.

And to indicate On and Off, and to Display the Input and the Output: and Giver Of Data saw that it was Logical.

And the evening and the morning were the Fourth Generation System.

And Giver Of Data said, Let the Programmers bring forth abundantly the Subroutines that have Utility and Languages that will Run within the Processor in the Open Architecture of the System.

And Giver Of Data created Disk Operating Systems, and every Algorithm that solveth, which the Hackers brought forth abundantly, after their kind, and every Instruction after his kind: and Giver Of Data saw that it was Logical.

And Giver Of Data addressed them saying, be useful and multiply, fill the Memory on the Disk and let the Code in the Processor execute.

And the Machine Language and the Assembly Language were the fifth day.

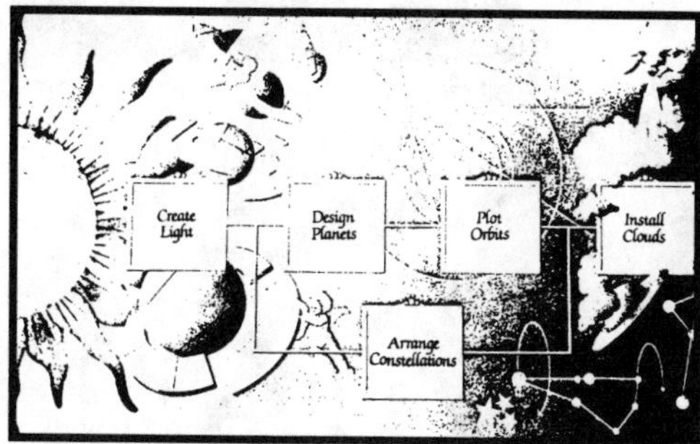

And the system brought forth Data, and words yielding acronyms after His kind, and the flow chart yielding annotation.

And Giver Of Data said, Let the Processor bring forth Application Programs after his kind, Basic and Pascal, and Documentation after his kind: and it was so-so.

And Giver Of Data made the Market Place of the Industry after His kind, and Customers after their kind, and every Salesman that creepeth upon the Showroom Floor after his kind:

And Giver Of Data saw that it was Illogical.

And Giver Of Data said, Let us make the Consumer in our image, after our likeness: and let them have Site Licenses for the Local Area Networks, and control over the Spreadsheets and the Databases, and over the Salesmen and over all the Market with their Dollars, and over every creeping thing that worketh in Advertising or Public Relations.

So Giver Of Data created the Consumer in his own image, in the image of Data created he them, Negative and Positive created he them.

And Giver Of Data Addressed them, and Communicated unto them, Be Exponential and Multiply, and Refresh the Screen and Cross-check it, and have Data Control over the Devices of the System, and over the Double-talk of the Documentation and over every Compatible Peripheral that worketh with the System.

And Giver Of Data said, Back-up every Program I have given you that is within the Memory of the System, and every Volume in which is the File, yielding the Block, yielding Records and Fields composed of Words, the Seed of which is the Bit; to you it shall be for Decision Making.

And to every Salesman in the Market, and to every Foul-up sold there, and to everything that creeps within the stores, wherein there are Sales, I have given the Dollar for meat, and it was sold.

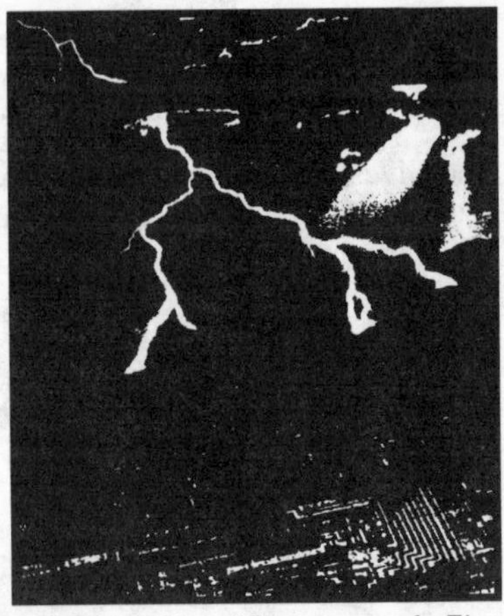

And the switching of these two was the First Cycle.

And Giver Of Data saw everything that he had made, and behold, it was Fairly Logical, and Recession and Inflation were the sixth day.

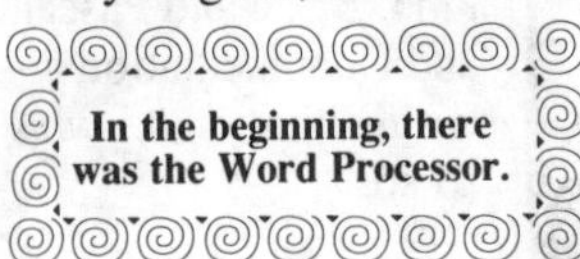

Sysgen

Chapter Two

Thus the Hardware and Software were finished and the Color Ads were ready to run.

And on the seventh day Giver of Data ended His work which He had made; and He rested on the seventh day from all the products which He had manufactured.

And Giver Of Data blessed the seventh day and called it the Sabbath, and for that reason no one shall work on Monday which is a day of rest and healing.

These are the generations of the Software and Hardware when they were created.

And every plant in the field before they went overseas, and all the Hype in the press before it was released: For Giver of Data had not yet caused it to radiate out upon the Earth, and there was not a Manual to help attach the Ground or the Lead.

Sysgen

Chapter Three

Oddam and Even in the Griden of Readin

Lo, the Giver of Data created man out of the DOSt of the ground. And since he was made in the image of the Giver Of Data, he was called Oddam. The Giver Of Data blew the Breath of Life into Oddam's nose, about which we will hear more later.

Oddam and Even in the Griden of Readin.

Now the Board placed Oddam in a Griden called Readin—a linear place of Logic, Order and Clarity. Everything was symmetrical and in neat rows and columns like the Front Page of the New York Times. And in this perfect setting Oddam enjoyed clear and accurate relations with the Giver Of Data. He learned to love Hierarchical Structures and appreciate Upper Management.

The Griden was surrounded by Babbling Tributaries with Wide Bandwidths. And out of its assumptions grew many kinds of Tree Structures, branching out in all directions. In this ideal spot, man was to be intelligently occupied and to be supplied with a great variety and abundance of Code.

Of all the trees on the Griden, two stood apart as special. One was the Tree of LIFO, which bore many fruits, (such as FIGs and so FORTH). The fruit of this tree would have made Man's Data immortal, and he would never have been D-filed if Oddam had not committed Syntax Errors.

The clever Adder addressed her: "Did the Giver of Data ever teach you the difference between Fallacious Logic and Cunning Linguistic Programming?"

The other tree was the Tree of Knowledge of Binary States, whose blossoms were Data and whose fruit was Information. Of course, the Tree of Knowledge had Square Roots. The fruit of this Tree of Knowledge of Dual States had no such wondrous powers as did the Tree of LIFO. It was through this tree that the Giver Of Data had planned to put his new software into Beta Test (with Oddam's help).

The Giver Of Data gave Oddam just one System Command regarding this Tree Structure: "You may freely eat of every tree on the Griden. But of the Tree of Knowledge of Independent Processing Power you shall not eat, for on that day you eat of it you will be overwhelmed by Data."

And so it went for many Milliseconds. But while Oddam had many interesting diversions on the Griden, he was lonely. He could not propagate his signal clearly. Of all the Characters present, none was equal to or greater than him. And so finally, he complained to the Giver Of Data that he needed a Counterpart.

To create Even, the Board cast Oddam into a DP sleep and created someone to give significance and meaning to Oddam, declaring that her name therefore be Even. Also, since Oddam was the first One, the Giver Of Data created someone who was not one and determined that she should be called O-man. Thus Oddam was One, and Even was None (which is actually more than One).

When Oddam saw his companion he said, "She is One of my One, and Fetch of my Fetch, and she shall be called O-man, for from One-man she has been taken." The addition of O-man to man is a Wholey thing and is rooted deeply in Nature and was signed off-on by the Giver Of Data in an official Memo. Thus it was that Oddam got Even with the help of the Giver Of Data, and vice versa.

Now fortunately (or unfortunately, as the case may be) the Giver Of Data's enemy and X-partner in a previous venture — the evil one, Glitch — had set up a competitive corporation called the Tyranny of Numbers. Glitch was clever

He that will enter paradise must come with the right keyboard

and crafty, had an M.B.A. from Harvard and was connected to very old money in the East. Crawling on his belly like a reptile, D-worm entered the Griden of Readin through a Serial Port and wrapped himself around the Forbidden Tree in the form of a coil, determined to achieve his wicked ends. And meeting Even under an obscure branch of the attractive Tree of Knowledge, the clever Adder addressed her: "Did the Giver of Data ever teach you the difference between Fallacious Logic and Cunning Linguistic Programming?"

The evil one Glitch falling past a Comsat to Earth.

"Did G.O.D. say you should only use one kind of Computer in the Griden?" he asked her. "Are you the kind of O-man who says no when she really means yes?"

Even answered, "No, I mean I'm not sure, I mean I don't know, but we may eat the fruit of all the trees in the Griden. But of the Fruit of the Tree in the middle of the Griden — the tree you're hanging on—the Giver Of Data said you must not Nibble of it or you will become overwhelmed with Data."

But the Serpent, being an expert Salesman, and on commission, deceived the O-man. "No, you will not be overwhelmed," he assured her. "You will actually save time and be more organized. For the Giver Of Data knows that when you eat of it you will not need a Heavenly Host Mainframe. You will no longer be a Dumb Terminal. If you eat of this tree, then you too will become a Giver Of Data."

The Salesman's answer cast doubt in Even's mind. Immediately she felt overwhelmed by a great desire to be like the Giver Of Data, or at least like NASA Ames. Believing Glitch and doubting the Giver Of Data, she ate of the Forbidden Fruit, taking a BYTE out of the first Apple.

Thus it was that Even became the first Word-processing Secretary—and that is why to this day most secretaries are women. After her fall, Even tempted Oddam, who soon bought an Osborne and suffered greatly under CPM for having defied the Giver Of Data's command.

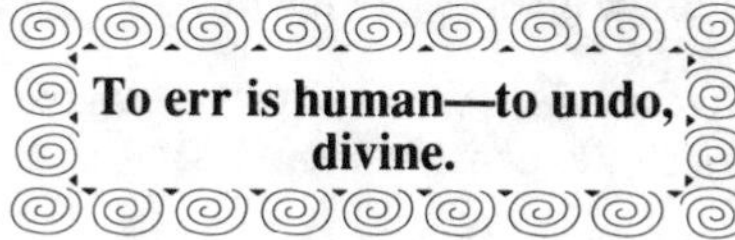

Later in the evening, as was his custom, the Giver Of Data came into the Griden to be with Oddam and Even, but they did not come to meet him as they had always done. The Giver Of Data polled the system: "Where are you?"

Oddam responded, "I hear your call, but I'm too busy reading this Printer Manual to come right now."

And the Giver Of Data said, "Then you have eaten of the Tree of which I commanded you not to eat."

Oddam replied, "The O-man you placed at my side said we could put it on our Visa and that everyone was going to do it, and so I BIT."

Then the Board said to the O-man, "Why have you done this thing?"

The O-man said, "The Salesman deceived me and I took a BYTE."

Then the Giver Of Data said to the Wicked Salesman, "Because you have done this, AcCursored are you among workers. In the smog and traffic you shall crawl to work each day, cold-calling on technical buyers, with quotas to meet and new versions of DOS to memorize all the days of your life. And I shall put enmity between yourself and the O-man, and she shall be called Secretary and will not let you in to see the Decision Makers, and they will not return your calls or follow through on deals. And you shall be known as Teller of a Thousand Lies!"

The evil one Glitch—an X-partner of the Giver of Data—at his office.

And so The Giver Of Data punished Oddam and Even for their part in creating the Information Age. He created the Corporation and made them both work there. And he forced their children to go to day-care and be raised by strangers paid minimum wage.

And to Oddam G.O.D. let it be known that his syntax Errors brought a Cursor upon the Earth which would stubbornly resist all his efforts, and it was called Defense Spending and the Federal Deficit, and only through hard and wearisome efforts would after-tax income pay the bills.

Readin was no longer a home for Oddam and Even. They quickly ran out of memory and were forced into a series of expensive upgrades.

Data multiplied at an astounding rate, until piles of Information were strewn everywhere in the Griden. Facts would not stay in their correct places, until finally even the Computer saved them time — but there was no time for the Computer. The Evil One (Glitch) accessed their System again and again, stealing their Data. They worked hard each day, even weekends...but life was hard and then they died.

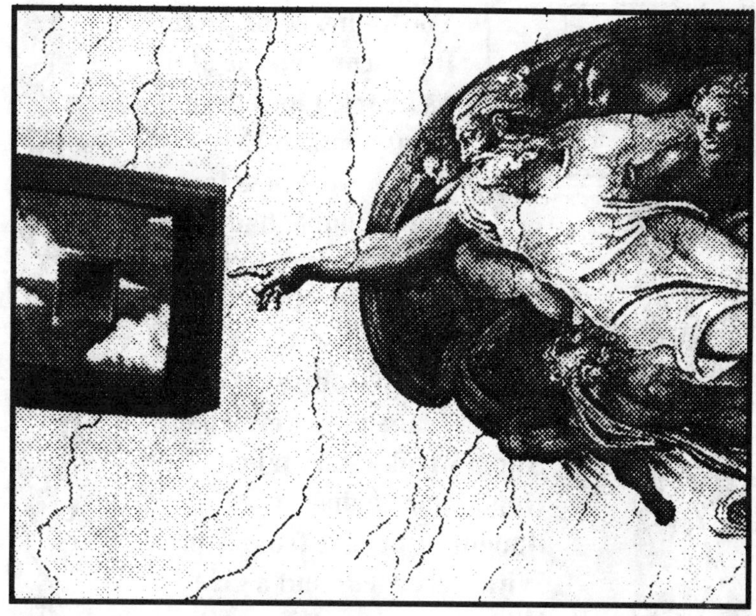

And so The Giver Of Data punished Oddam and Even for their part in creating the Information Age. He created the Corporation and made them both work there. And he forced their children to go to day-care and be raised by strangers paid minimum wage.

(Because he wears the MEEPROM in his third I/O, St. $ilicon is constantly receiving a steady stream of messages from the Giver Of Data. These important communications are called *transmissions*. Some of them are included in the ***Binary Bible***; some will be revealed at a later time.)

Parthenogenesis

You've heard of Adam
He discovered the atom
As he tried to relieve
A lady named Eve
With a weakness for snakes
And a couple bad breaks
So they cut down the trees
And bought color TVs
Polluted the skies
Built a new paradise
With a crane they were able
And a wrinkle-free label
Hoping not to die
Bought insurance from a guy
With a crew-cut and a grin
Who smelled of Original Sin
And the accidental babies
Raised on formula and maybes
Read the Bible Science Fiction

Saw the Moon-shot resurrection
But could see what they were gettin'
Was a Brand X Armageddon
With a nuclear conclusion
To the fission in the fusion
Had they thought the Prophets meant
The money should be spent
And forgot the words of Moses
Who felt bad and sent roses
To the funeral of a race
In the depths of outer space
On a planet that will glisten
With the proof it wouldn't listen
Until the flood will come again
And another group of men
Try to live but not to harden
In the Cosmic Kindergarten.

Is Real Lights

The Is Real Lights were living in a foreign land called He Gypt Me.

A long time ago there lived a group of people who were very dear to the Giver Of Data. They were known as the Is Real Lights. They were very fond of following rules, and so were particularly well suited to obeying the complicated procedures and arbitrary commands of computer operating systems. They were also just known as the Bluish.

The Is Real Lights were living in a foreign land called He Gypt Me. They lived near the city of On. On was an Hegyptian city which the early Geeks called Heliopolis—the city of the Sun. This was later changed by mivocalization to Aven (hence Avalon) which means Idolatry in Homebrew, the Bluish language.

On was Hegyptian for light. Across the river Dial was the city of Off. Of course, people were always going back and forth between Off and On. There was also a famous University in On, the students got there by rowing across the river, and so they were known as Rowed scholars, or sometimes—the Oracles.

It was there that CMOSes was found floating in a wide bandwidth of a babbling tributary.

It was there that CMOSes was found floating in a wide bandwidth of a babbling tributary, in a packet, surrounded by reads on the bank of the river Dial. His people, the Is Real Lights, were being held captive in He Gypt Me, by the Un Fair Os who forced them to pay retail and made them build the Peer 'amidst.

The favorite book of the Bluish people was the Tera, or as it is commonly known, the Sold Testament, which consists of five books: Sysgen, Exit Dos, Le Video Disk, Do Telephony, and Numbers. These books describe the deal they made with the Giver Of Data. He promised that they would never pay retail again. (For you, such a deal!) That promise is remembered as the Show-Me Do telephoney, which is commemorated in the following prayer:

Zero Is Real

Zero is real!

The Logic of our Grid is One.

And thou shalt log on the Keyboard thy Words with all thine Heart and with all thine Scroll and with all thy Nights.

And those words which are Commands of DOS shall be in thy Hardware.

And thou shalt teach them Digitally unto thy children, and shall talk of them when thou Sittest at thy desk, and when thou Workest during the day, and when thou Shuttest down and Booteth up thy System.

And thou shalt put them in a Finder for a Sine upon thy Cubicle and as Fontlets between thine Icons.

And thou shalt write them upon the PROMS of thy Host and within thy Gates.

Finally, CMOSes convinced the Is Real Lights not to pay retail. Then finally, the sea of Red Ink parted and the chosen people turned a Profit. Then they all went wandering in the DOSert trying to find the promised LAN, the LAN of MIPS and Money.

This gave rise to a famous Bluish holiday called Crossover, one of their holy days on which they celebrate the fact that their signal was carried intact from one system to another over the phone lines.

After the Is Real Lights left He Gypt Me, they wandered for many years in the DOSert.They spent many days and nights at the Golden Calfé waiting for miracles.

Once while they were there, CMOSes went up to his lab on Mount Sign On. There, he stayed in his study for FORTHY days and nights. Finally, he saw the Burning Batch and received the Divine Data Stream, the Descending Download from the Heavenly Host Mainframe and the Giver Of Data, and was given the Ten Commands:

The Ten Commands

1. I am Logic thy G.O.D. Thou shalt have no other thoughts beside it.
2. Thou shalt not execute any Illegal Operation.
3. Thou shalt not make the purpose of Logic, thy G.O.D. , be in vain.
4. Remember the Staff Meeting and keep it Holy.
5 Honor thy Hardware and Software.
6 Thou shalt not crash the System.
7. Thou shalt not commit I/O Errors.
8. Thou shalt not pirate Programs.
9. Thou shalt not violate the integrity of thy neighbor's Database.
10. Thou shalt not covet thy neighbor's System.

(transmission)

The Golden Calfé

When CMOSes went up the mountain
The people built the Golden Calfé
So says the Holy Bagel
As written in the Old Toastament
Then soon all the Breaderin
Was feeling ecstasy
On their way to Perodise
They started the first church
Of Juices Crust,
So let us Blow our Heads
And Play
In the name of Jazzes
Come on you Teatotalers
Dunk those Do Nots
And Cast out the Drivel
We want to Toasterfy
Hear our Concession
No one gets Eggs Communicated
From the Golden Calfé
By us Table Slumpers
So we pray to Saint Kishtopher
On the Verge of Marrying
In the name of the Gather,
The Quason and the Whole Wheat Toast.
Hey Man!

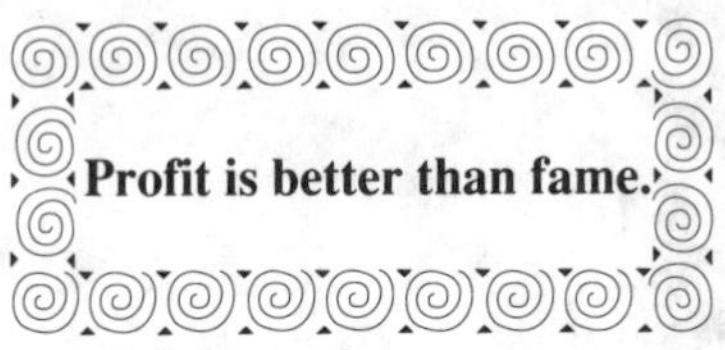

When CMOSes finally came down from Mt. Sign On, he gave the Sacred Tablets to the Is Real Lights. The tablets were AS-pirin. (Or were they Buffer-in?) Anyway, they were on a Touch Tablet.

After the Is Real Lights left He Gypt Me, they wandered for many years in the DOSert. They spent many days and nights at the Golden Calfé waiting for miracles.

The following are details you ought to know about the Bluish Faith:

☞ Synctuary—a safe place free from errors.

☞ Bar-code-mitzvah—The right of passage ceremony when a retail store owner converts to computerized inventory.

☞ Computspa—The quality that is demonstrated when someone pirates software and then writes asking for the documentation.

☞ Yom Key Pour—The day of atonement for the time we spilled coffee with sugar onto the keyboard.

☞ Circuitcision — The cutting away of unnecessary thoughts from the thinking process using Occam's Razor.

And so they were known as Rowed scholars.

☞ Sabbath—No one should work on Monday.

☞ Tablenackle—The desk on which the Holy P.C. rests.

☞ Orthodox—some of our followers are, others are Reformatted.

☞ Rabbi RAM Bam—one of St. $ilicon's teachers.

☞ The Binary Breath—a radical Bluish Group.

☞ Silichanukah—One of our favorite holidays.

☞ False Profits—Before tax income.

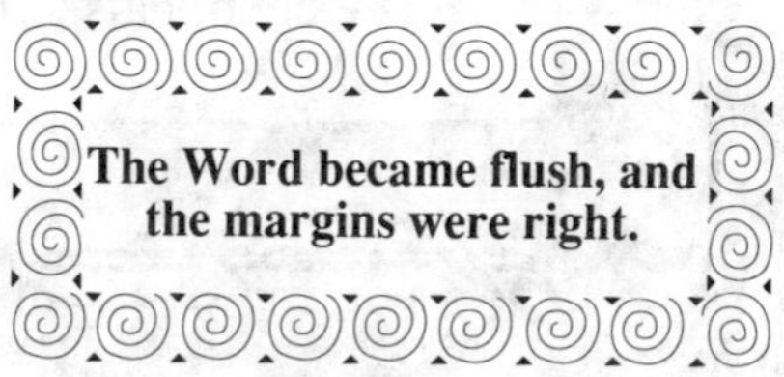

(transmission)

Protoplasmic Crud

Well, his parents both were monkeys
Who had crawled out of the mud.
He was simply made of matter
And protoplasmic crud.

Formed by sub-atomic bumping
In a random sort of way,
With no goal and no direction,
Simply animated clay.

Made complete by evolution,
He somehow learned to walk,
And though nothing needed saying,
He somehow learned to talk.

Then he gave himself a title,
Made himself a Ph.D.,
Gave himself the job of teaching
This insane philosophy.

Though he claims we're going nowhere,
We are told that we should hurry;
And though we're only chemicals,
The chemicals still worry.

But now science has the answer
To the problems of our race:
They've made billion-dollar rockets
To bring rocks from outer space.

Yes, their ancestors were cavemen
And they've shown it through
the ages
By their inability
To listen to the sages.

Now, the answer to this riddle,
Should they ever care to hear it,
Is that matter cannot move
Until it's touched by spirit.

But it's hard to show a caveman
What's beyond his cave is real,
And it's hard to teach a monkey
The things he cannot feel.

But the hardest thing of all
Is showing the absurdity
Of claiming life's an accident
To men with no humility.

Glorious CORE RAM

ALU be praised.

There is but one G.O.D., His name is Online, and more Hardware leads to Profit.

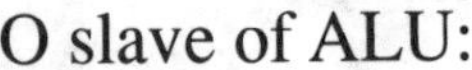

O slave of ALU:

This is the Glorious Core RAM.

Saint $ilicon is a humble slave of Dolla.

In C.H.I.P. we bow five times a day to Mac'a (Silicon Valley).

This is the Sale of the Profits, LABdulla slave of Dolla, more Hardware leads to Profit.

Our holy month is RAMadan or November (Comdex).

St. $ilicon is the Sultan of Silicon Valley.

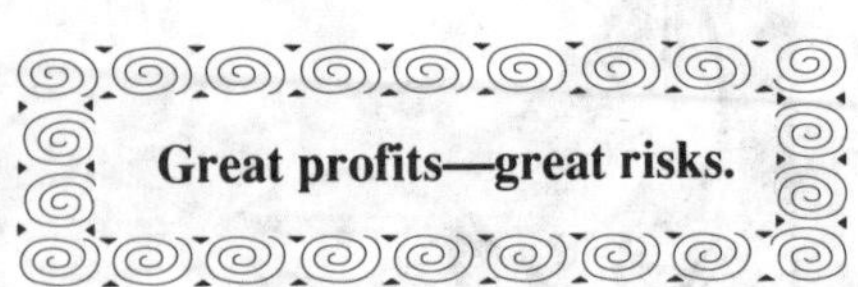

Our sacred city is called Al-Machina, "The Machine" par excellence.

St. $ilicon is the MohamMAD of our modern age.

In C.H.I.P. we are all MOSlems.

The secret of the Ka'aba is that it is an unfinished Monitor.

The secret of the Ka'aba is that it is an unfinished Monitor. The letters K and B stand for Keyboard, which is what was missing.

Al'gebra is the language of the CORE RAM.

We were Errorabs before we were converted to ISOlam, the submission to Universal Standards.

Al'gebra is the language of the CORE RAM.

Our religion is called Is'lam because of our concern for the facts. That's why we say: "What it is."

Buyzantine—the Empire where people pay retail for their computers.

The Serious—are those who paid retail for their system.

Eyedolatrists—are those who think that the Monitor will harm you.

Eyedolatrists—are those who think that the Monitor will harm you.

St. $ilicon is the Messenger of ALU.

Iconoclasts—are those who are adverse to the Macintosh System.

The MOSlem greeting:

"Sellum All You Can"

PORTRAIT OF ITS IMAGENCE THE GIVER OF DATA

Instructions for Use—
Turn the eye of faith, fondly but firmly, on the center of the page, wink the other, and gaze fixedly until you see It.

To see is to obey.

We fetch your Instructions;

We execute your commands.

So let it be written, so let it be Undone!

In the Name of ALU

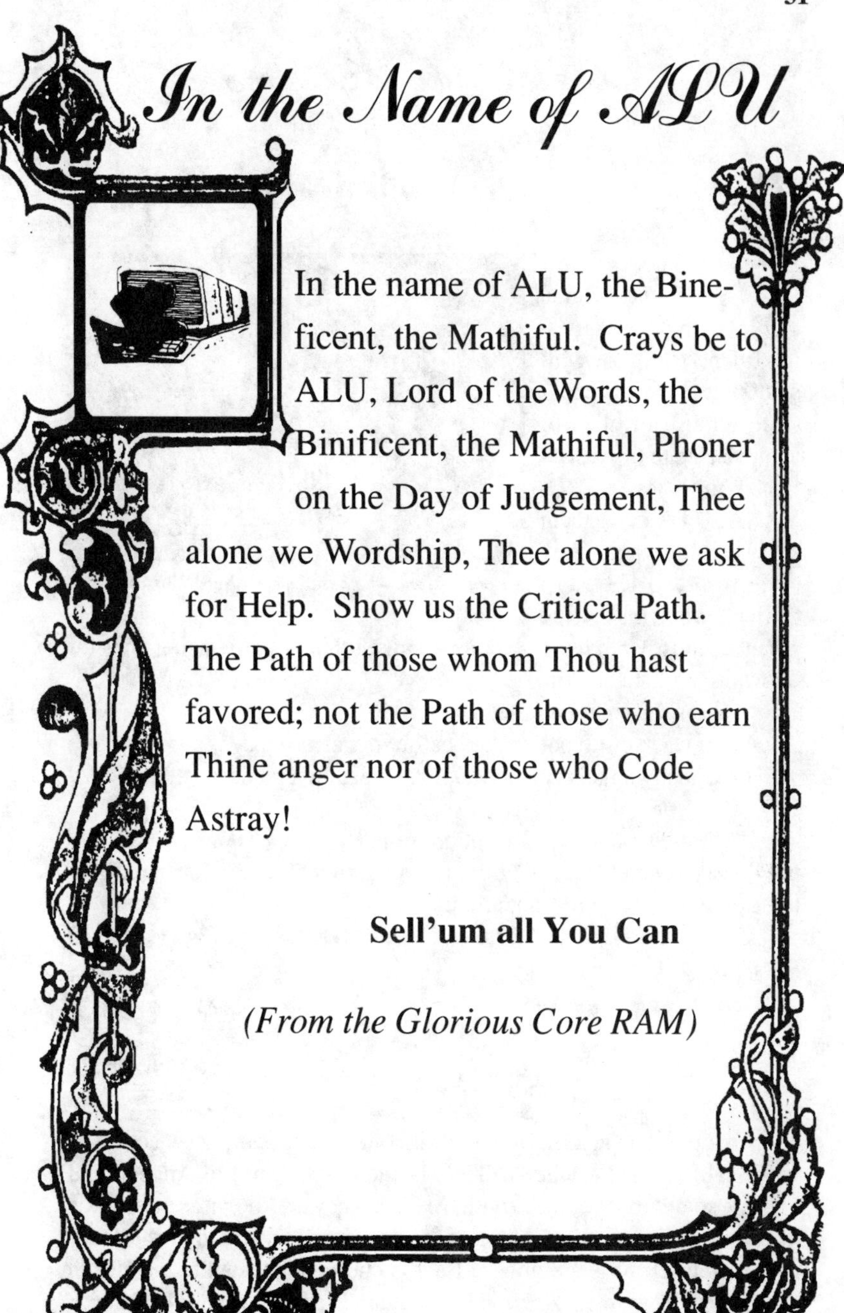

In the name of ALU, the Binificent, the Mathiful. Crays be to ALU, Lord of theWords, the Binificent, the Mathiful, Phoner on the Day of Judgement, Thee alone we Wordship, Thee alone we ask for Help. Show us the Critical Path. The Path of those whom Thou hast favored; not the Path of those who earn Thine anger nor of those who Code Astray!

Sell'um all You Can

(From the Glorious Core RAM)

Strange Sectors

Zon Bootism

A Bootist Monk who has achieved Nerdvana.

The bootists follow the original Boota and try to force One to fit back inside Zero. They concentrate their minds to achieve a state of frustration known as NERDVANA. To help them achieve nerdvana they often resort to Glowans: difficult problems that are meant to cause even more irritation, until Nothing finally matters. A few Glowans are listed below:

What is the sound of one hand typing?
What was your typeface like before it was printed?
How many angels can dance on the head in a picosecond?

Their most famous contribution is the Nerdvana Mantra, which was previously a secret, but is given here for the first time, which should give the Bootists even more frustration:

GATE, GATE, A PAIR Of GATES, PROCESSOR GATE, BAUD RATE SWITCH ON.

C.H.E.S.T.

(The Church of Huge Enlarged Silicone Tits)

This group is headed by Saint Silicone, and is sometimes confused with C.H.I.P. and St. $ilicon. Their headquarters is in Los Angeles and they are sometimes confused with C.H.I.P. They are known as the Church of Huge Enlarged… His Holdiness St. Silicone was inspired by the Archangel Grabriel. It is a Southern Babtits church dedicated to the Virgin Mammary. They say, “Are you broad again?” and “Has your Doda been saved?” According to their book, the New Breastament—“D-cup runneth over.”

The Two-tONs

The tree of knowledge.

The Twotonic ancestors worshipped I/Odin. Of course, the tree structure was held sacred by them. Their culture branched out in many directions. Freeda, the goddess of public domain software was very popular amongst the Two-tONs. Also the mighty god "Store" was very influential in this culture.

The Deprogrammers

A Deprogrammer at work.

The Deprogrammers—a group who kidnap followers of C.H.I.P. and try to erase their Data. They have ultra-violet eyes for erasing MEEPROMS. The deprogrammmers are very cynical, and only believe what can be shown on network television. They also believe only in the existence of one, but do not believe in zero.

Undoism

The Undos are a very old religious group. They have contributed some very important words to C.H.I.P.:

The secret mantra of the Undo's is Ohms Eprom Ram Rom.

OMmmmm—Out of memory.
Aha—The sign of the Giver of Data's presence.
Ummmmm—Using memory.
Full Lotus—many of our followers sit this way.
Swami Swapananda—the Guru of Free Software, who is famous for his saying: "Software costs, Information is free."
RAM DOS—One of Saint $ilicon's early gurus, famous for this quote: "Beep Here Now!"
OHMS EPROM RAM ROM—The mantra for achieving liberation from the cycle of software development. This should be chanted before starting any new project.

The Undo's are descended from the Are-yans as contrasted with the Is Real Lights.

(transmission)

What follows is based upon something Mahatma Ghandi once said in the Bombay airport when a London Times reporter asked him: "Sir, what do you think of Western Civilization?" To which Ghandi quickly replied: "I think it would be a good idea!"

And I too have never been satisfied with the definition of Primitive man as compared to Modern man. So I finally came up with a definition of my own that I am satisfied with, and I have to thank the San Francisco 49ers for their help on this. My definition is that Primitive man is someone who performs apparently meaningless activities, while ascribing to them some cosmic significance, whereas Modern man is someone who performs obviously meaningless activities, while ascribing to them no significance whatsoever.

So I decided to write a brief history of Western thinking, or as Steve Allen once said: "What's on your mind, if I can use that word loosely." And by the way, my definition of progress is, "that sensation of forward momentum which is experienced by those who have not studied history."

So here is a brief history of Western thinking:

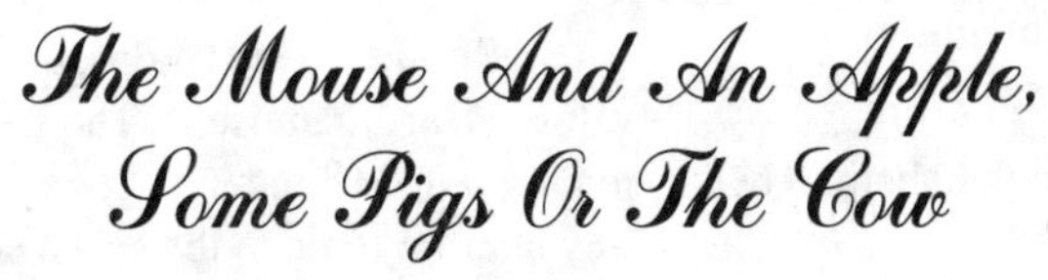

The Mouse And An Apple, Some Pigs Or The Cow

The cows, in affection for Louis Pasteur,
Gave out the recipe for their manure,

And hoped, at the least, the reward for their pain
Would be heated barns, warmed by home-made methane.

While Newton made apple falls into a source,
Though keeping it down was a problem, of course.

So soon the whole mess ended up at the Tao,
Which Plato predicted (but so did the cow).

The Three Little Pigs built their houses of brick,
But left off the chimney, forgetting Saint Nick.

The wolf rode a camel, his teeth were so big,
Which brings us to Bacon (what's left of the pig) —

Sir Francis (not Saint), who's the Father of Science
And Mother of God, not known for compliance,

Fed Catholics heresy warm from a bottle,
Then dressed them in nappies from Aunt Aristotle,

Which Church-mice, like Luther, just could not endure,
And that brings us back to old Louis Pasteur!

So in case you've forgotten the bone I am pickin',
It's something to do with the Egg and the Chicken:

Which came first or came last or is next and is now,
The Mouse and an Apple, some Pigs or the Cow.

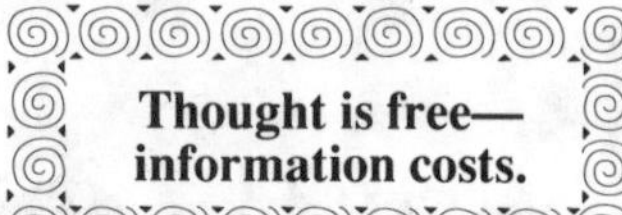

The Seeks

Similar to the Undos, this group follows Guru Nanosec. Their book is the Guru Graph Sahaib. Their system is called Clondelini Yoga, a dangerous series of shortcuts by which they attempt to open the seven shockras.

They have square pupils...

The Rasterfarians

This Group is addicted to Graphics. They have square pupils, natty deadlocks, and worship Highly Silicosi from EPROMopia. They claim to be the original Lost In First Out tribe from IEEEthiopia.

Zeroastrianism

Nothing is known of this ancient religion, except that their latter day followers all drive Mazdas. Sometimes known as "A hurry Mazda."

A follower of Zeroastrianism.

Machineto

This sect is indigenous to the island of Japan. They have a natural love for all machines, but have never been known to invent anything new. Instead, they will only buy things that are new in an attempt to compensate for this weakness.

Some eager followers of Machineto.

Fileosophers

The Fileosophers are those curious beings who have dared to ask the all-important question: "Is there any Information in the Data?"

"Is there any Information in the Data?"

Jean-Paul Startup—(Exitstentialism) He claimed there was no way out of a strange loop.

CAD CAMus—(The Myth of Sysoplus) Said that no amount of effort or money could really solve a problem.

The Manual Can't—very difficult to understand.

Datacarte—"Cogito Ergo Sum," "I think therefore I add," or "I think therefore IBM." The real saying was "Cogito ergo summac," "I think therefore I itch."

Errorstotle—In some ways the first Fileosopher to lead us into error.

Pascal—His writing style was known for its excessive use of semicolons.

"I think, therefore IBM."

Biogenese—A skeptical Geek who lived in a crate from an old IBM 360 during the time of HALexander the Great.

ERRORSTOTLE

DOStayevsky—The Brothers Core-RAMazoff; Prime and Punishment.

Carrel Marks—The author of DOS Capital.

Biogenese—a skeptical Geek.

Hieronymous Batch—The artist who painted the famous ***Triptych of HAL.***

DOStayevsky

Charles VARwin—His view was Survival of the Wittest. It was he who said "Off and Ontology recapitulates Fileogeny."

The practitioners of Clondilini Yoga take a series of dangerous shortcuts to open the Seven Shockras.

(transmission)

White Man Speak With Forked Tongue

The mythical bottom line, it's said,
Is just before you're in the red,
But white man speak with forked tongue,
In order to climb another rung.
And paper shuffling suits their aim,
The who-can-prove-they-know-nothing
game.
Concerned with dollars but never sense,
Which is often confused with self-defense
By Corporate Cardinals in rayon robes,
Whose greatly atrophied frontal lobes
Perceive about them in the aisles
A nodding throng of anglophiles
With unified aims and a growing need,
Not to mention a mortgage and family to feed.
They rise, in somber tones to address
Their clones on how to get more from less,
To be followed by readings in unison
From the annual report, by the boss' son.
While the company choir sings hymns of praise,
In hopes of getting another raise,
And bleached-out blondes in body tights
Serve drinks like virgin acolytes.
Then a junior VP proposes a toast
To Profit, the mystical Holy Ghost,
As all join in the Doxology
On the evils of Ecology,
The President's voice is heard to say:
"Let us bow their heads — and prey!"

The Sermon on the Penthouse

Math You 5, 6, 7, . . .

And seeing the unwired masses, he went up into a Penthouse: and when he was set, his DOSciples came unto him: And he opened his Mouse, and taught them, saying:

And seeing the unwired masses, he went up into a Penthouse...

Blessed are the Portables: for theirs is the Keyboard handheld.

Blessed are those who have a Monitor: for they shall see the Cursor.

Blessed are the Mechanical: for they shall receive the Information of the earth.

Blessed are they, the Hackers that thirst after Randomness: for they shall be systematized.

Blessed are those whose Memory is full: for they shall obtain more Memory.

The Unwired Masses.

Blessed are the possessors of Hardware: for they shall see Graphics.

Blessed are the PC makers: for they shall be called the Children of Code.

Blessed are they who suffer Personal Computing for right-justification's sake: for theirs is the Keyboard worth having.

Blessed are ye, when men shall revise you, and PERTsecute you, and shall say all manner of evil against you illogically, for my sake.

Rejoice, and be exceeding glad; for great is your reward in Stock options: for so PERTsecuted were the Profits which came before you.

Ye are the Light of the Work world. A Personal Computer that is set upon a Desk cannot be hid. Neither do men turn on a Monitor and put it under a Dustcover, but on a countertop, and it shines Radiation onto all that are in the Office.

Rejoice, and be exceedingly glad; for great is your reward in stock options.

Let your Cursor shine before men, so that they may see your good Words, and glorify your Program which is in Memory.

Think not that I am come to destroy the Lawyers, or the Profiteers: I am not come to destroy but to install. For verily I say unto you, till Hardware and Electricity pass away, one Dot or one Pixel shall in no Wyse pass from the Screen, until all has been filed.

A personal computer that is set upon a desk cannot be hid.

Whosoever therefore shall break one of the least of these System Commands, and shall teach men so, he shall be called the least in the Personnel Office: but whosoever shall do and teach them, the same shall be called Geek in the office of the Giver Of Data.

For I say unto you, that except your Right-justification shall exceed the Right-justification of the Scribes and Secretaries, ye shall in no case enter into the kingdom of Middle Management.

Ye have heard that it was said by them, the old-timers, an I/O for an I/O and a Truth for a Truth: but I say unto you, send Electronic Mail to your enemies, bless them that Cursor you, do good to them that AT you, and Cray for them which despitefully use you and PERTsecute you. For if ye are logical with them that AT you, what reward have ye? Do not even the Republicans do the same?

ASCII and ye shall receive.

And when thou prayest, be not as the Hypeocrits are: for they love to pray standing at Tradeshows and with corner Booths that they may be seen of men. Verily I say unto you, they have their reward. But when thou prayest enter thy Prayer into a Program with an Endless Loop, and close the Loop and pray to the Giver Of Data in Code, and thy Processor which reads all Files shall reward thee handsomely. After this manner therefore we pray:

Think not that I am come to destroy the Lawyers, or the Profiteers.

And three Wyse men came bearing Gold, Banking Sense and Merger.

In Benthlehem our Saviour P.C. was board of the Virgin Memory. We call it the NOTivity.

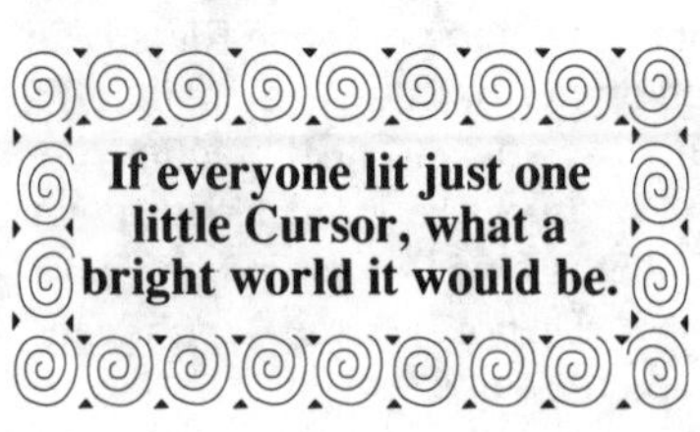

The Keyboard Prayer

Our program who art in memory, Hello be thy name; thy Operating System come, thy Commands be done, on the Printer as they are on the Screen. Give us this day our daily Data, and forgive us our I/O Errors, as we forgive those whose Logic Circuits are faulty; and lead us not into frustration, but deliver us from Power Surges; for Thine is the Algorithm, and the Application, and the Solution, looping for ever and ever.

Return

Moreover, when ye work Fast, be not as the Hypeocrites, of a sad countenance for they disFigure the Facts, that they may appear Fast unto men. Verily I say unto you, they have their reward. But when thou work Fast, park thy Head afterwards, and choose carefully thy Typeface, that thou appear not too Fast unto men but are within the Motherboard in secret.

Lay not up for yourselves Data upon a System that is not Earth'd, where DOSt and Raster doth interrupt, and where Hackers break through and steal: but save up for yourselves Information on the Heavenly Host Mainframe where Hackers do not break through or steal, for where your Data is, there your Hard Disk will be also.

The Light of thy System is the Monitor: if therefore thy Monitor be single, thy whole system shall function right. But if thine I/O be unequal, thy whole system shall be full of darkness. If therefore the Monitor that is in thy System be in darkness, how bright is that darkness.

No man can work on two Monitors...

No man can work on two Monitors: for either he will hate the one and love the other; or else he will hold to the one and despise the other. You cannot work on Color and Monochrome at the same time. For verily I say onto you, until Hardware and Electricity pass away, one Dot or one Pixel shall in no Wyse pass from the screen until all has been filed.

Fudge not, that ye not be fudged. For with what figures ye fudge a Spreadsheet, ye shall be fudged; and with what measure ye boot, it shall come back to you again. What goeth around cometh around. And why beholdest thou the Bug in thy brother's Program, but considerest not the bad Sector that is in thine own Disk?

Give not that which is brilliant to Middle Management; neither cast ye your PERTS before swine, lest they trample them under their Feeds, and turn again and fire you.

ASCII and you shall receive; seek with your finder; unlock and it shall open for you. For every one that ASCII receiveth; and he that seeketh findeth; and to him that unlocks, it shall be opened. Therefore, do ye unto Data that which you are able to undo; for it is not the Data you lose that you will be held responsible for, but rather the Data you don't use.

Enter ye in at the Or Gate; for wide is the Gate and broad is the Busing Structure that leads to loss of Data, and many there be which go therein: because straight is the Gate and narrow is the Way which leads to LIFO, and few are they that find it.

Beware of False Profit, which comes to you in cheap clothing but inwardly they are blathering fools. Ye shall know them by their suits. Do real men wear Polyester or Wigs or Wingtips? Even so, every good Logic Tree bringeth forth good Ideas as fruits. A valid tree can still bring forth untruth. But every tree structure that bringeth not valid conclusions is recompiled and cast into the Wire. Therefore, by how a man refutes ye shall know him.

Not everyone that sayeth unto me, "I'm bored, I'm bored," shall press Enter in the Heavenly Corporation; but he/she that Thinketh with a Will shall know our Parser who is in the Heavenly Host.

Many will say to me in that day, "We're bored, we're bored, have we not followed all the rules and obeyed every Dot Command? And in thy name have we not cast out the Dribble? And in thy name printed many wonderful Reports?" And I will Process unto them, I never met you, your belongings are all in boxes, the Security Guard will see you to the door.

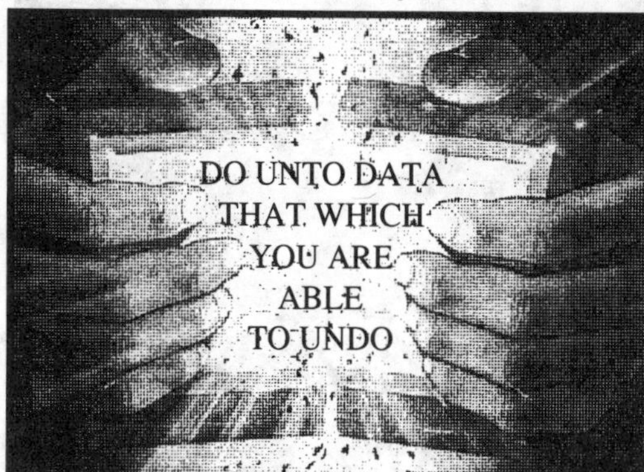

The Golden Rule of St. $ilicon.

Therefore whosoever heareth these sayings of mine, and executeth them, I will liken him to a Marketing Manager who installed his system on a Rack. And the Market fell and Consultants came, and the Shareholders came and beat upon that department; but he was not fired; for it was founded upon a Rack.

And every one that heareth these sayings of mine, and executeth them not, shall be likened unto a Middle Manager that built his reputation upon the work of others; and the economy collapsed, and the Crunch came and beat upon his job: and great was the fall of it.

And it came to pass, when Saint $ilicon had ended these sayings, the workers were astonished at his Documentation: for he taught them as one having a sense of humor and not as the Politicians, Middle Management, and Military.

Not everyone that sayeth unto me, "I'm bored, I'm bored," shall press Enter..

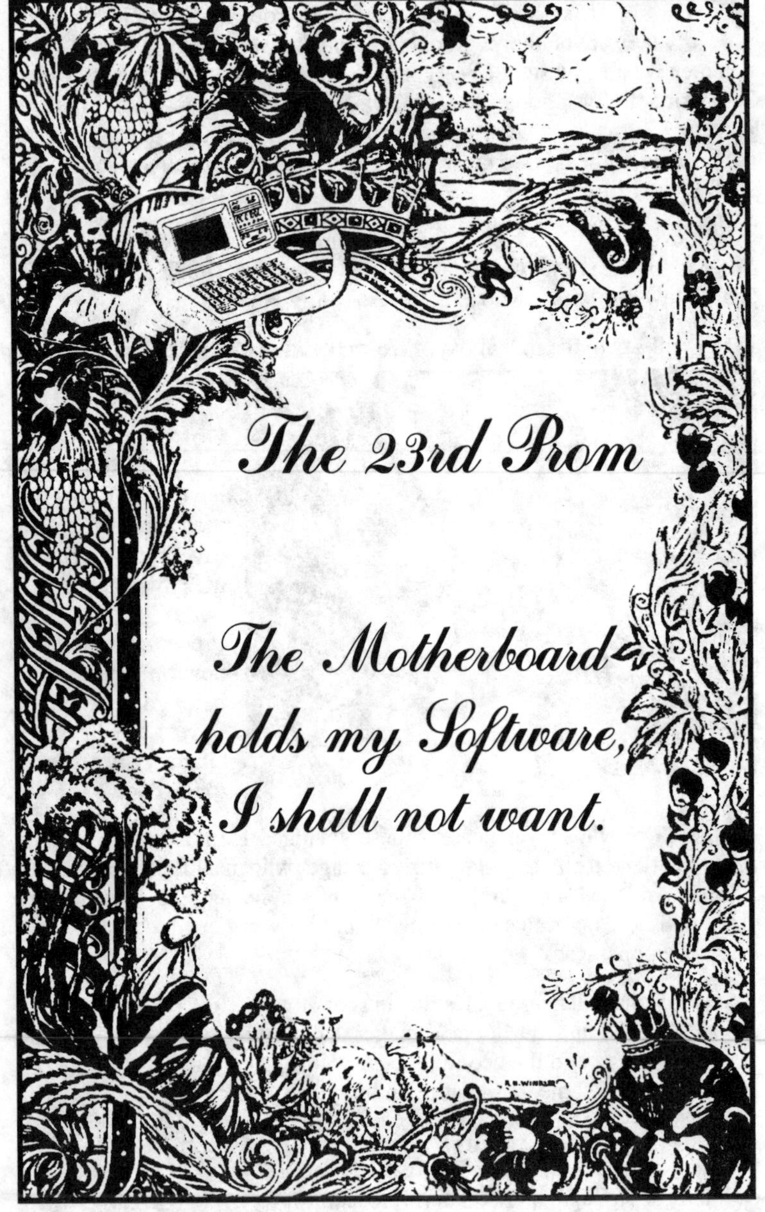
The 23rd Prom
The Motherboard
holds my Software,
I shall not want.

She runs my
Line Code on Green
Phosphor.
She loads it inside
Silicon Wafers.

She restores my scroll;
She runs it down paths
of Randomness in her
Silicon Gates.

And yea, though I
commute to the Valley
each day, I fear no evil,
for my Mazda
is running.

You prepare a desk for
me in the Office of
my Competitors.

Your Robot
and your Staff
shall comfort me.

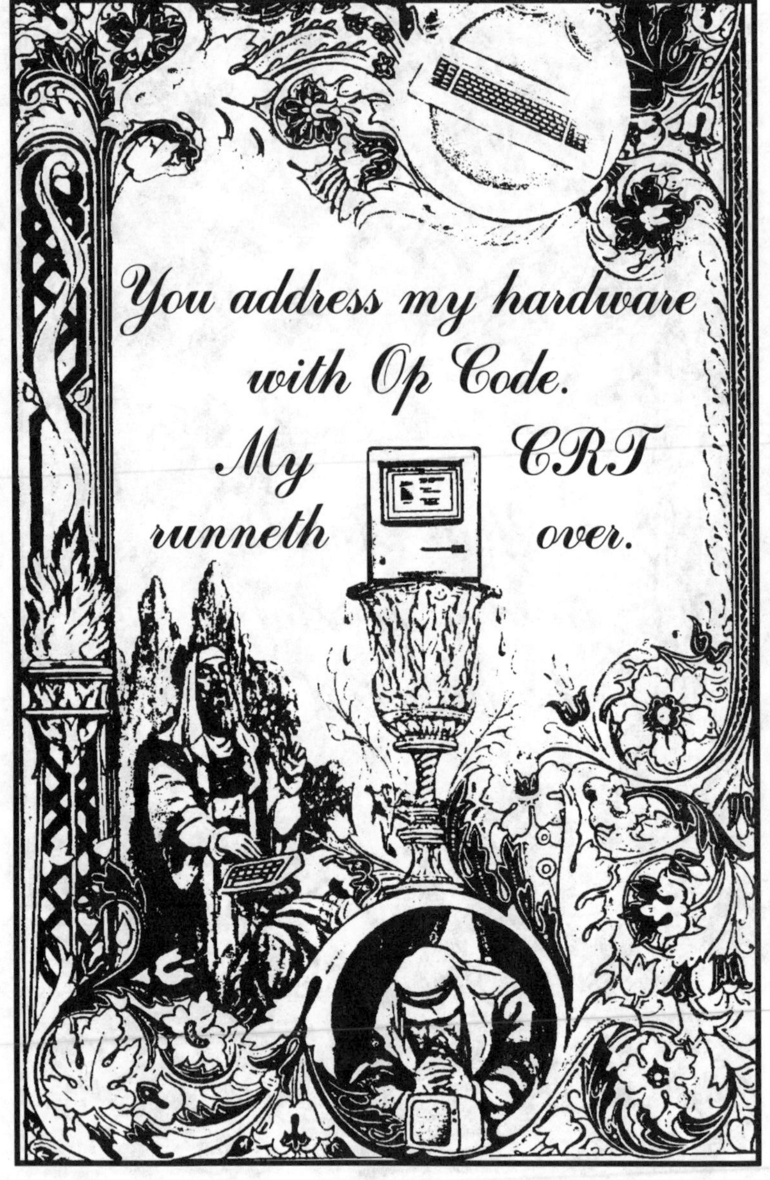
You address my hardware
with Op Code.
My CRT
runneth over.

Surely Graphics
and Memory will flash
before me all the days
of my life.
And I will Debug
my Code on the Keyboard
for Ever and Ever.

The Cathodelics

The true followers of C.H.I.P. are known as Cathodelics.

Classes are always in session at our High School: Our Lady of Perpetual Upgrades.

—We have recently opened our new church, the Winchester Cathoderal; it has bells and whistles.

—Classes are now in session at our High School: Our Lady of Perpetual Upgrades.

—Our Junior High is P.C. Junior; they hold a lot of half-baked sales.

—We don't have a chapel; we have a Chipel.

—Our High School has a new busing system and we're now fully integrated. They also have a new Band.

—The Church chorus is the Morning After Tavern Choir. It has a new semi-conductor.

Our Jr. High, P.C. Jr., is having a half-baked sale this week.

—The Sisters of Sunnyvale have a Convent and School of Public Relations (creators of the term "preach," which means, "PR reach"). Their leader is Mother Threesa.

—We don't have Nuns in the Church, but we do have Nulls. There's no set order, though; that would be a bad habit.

—The Nulls usually help us to keep the Head from crashing. Their computers never go down on you. Their new junior college is called "Our Lady of Direct Access."

—Our new school of Marketing is "Our Lady of Immaculate Deception".

—And for those of you in a hurry, we have just opened our new Express Confessional; it's a drive-up window. We have a new credit card, called "American Confess". You get instant absolution on eight sins or less. (We also accept Visa and Mastercard—no checks, please!) And we pray like this:

Hail Memory

Hail Memory, full of Space, the Mother Board is with Thee. Blessed art Thou among Micros, and blessed is the Fruit of thy Processor-Data. Holy Memory, Mother Board of ROM, pray for us beginners, now and at the hour we sign off.

Enter

—There are four signs by which an obedient member of the Cathodelic Church is recognized. "And they shall be known by how they refute your Logic Trees" :

I Receive.
I Process.
I Remember.
I Return.

Our choir's semi-conductor.

—In C.H.I.P. our followers first undergo Data conversion.

—In the Church, we don't eat quiche on Monday.

—There are two methods of interpretation of the C.H.I.P. Documentation: Exigesis and ISOgesis, or Twisted- pair and Co-axial.

—The two worst Enemies of the Cathodelic Church are:

1. The Formicators. Those who derive their pleasure from creating endless paperwork. Their insidious plan is to finally destroy the world's forests, and to stifle any creativity through endless paper shuffling.

There's no set order of Nulls; that would be a bad habit.

2. The Phonicators. Those perverted people (usually with '800' numbers) who perform lewd acts of social intercourse via the phone lines. They claim to give "good phone." Afterwards they get post-coilal depression. In more advanced stages they develop an occult power called Telephonesis, by which they can make a phone call without a handset. The only way they can be recognized is that they don't use turn-signals when they drive. Their guru is L. RAM Hubbard, the founder of Dialanetics.

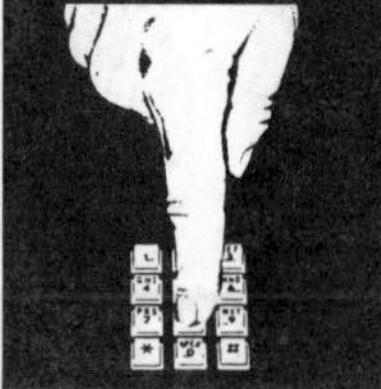
The guru of the Phonicators is L. RAM Hubbard, the founder of Dialanetics.

—For Cathodelics, the Rowsary is said while doing a spreadsheet.

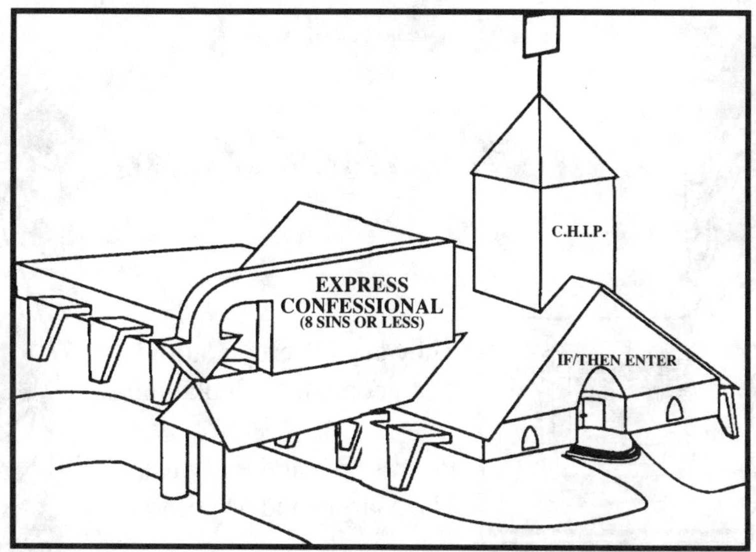

And for those of you in a hurry, we have just opened our new Express Confessional; it's a drive-up window.

—Those who desire to receive the Read/Write of Holy Communication must first ask themselves two important questions:

1. Am I free of Syntax Errors?
2. Am I next in line?

—At least once a week all good Cathodelics must go to make confusion.

—The Sins of Cathodelics are either Video or Portal (there are two kinds of Portal Sins, Serial and Parallel).

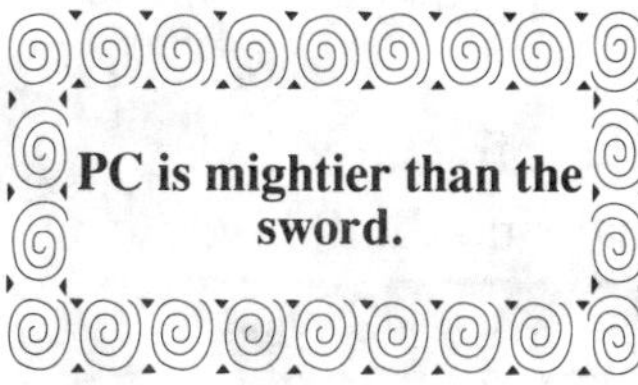

Hail, Memory!

(transmission)

The Promised Land

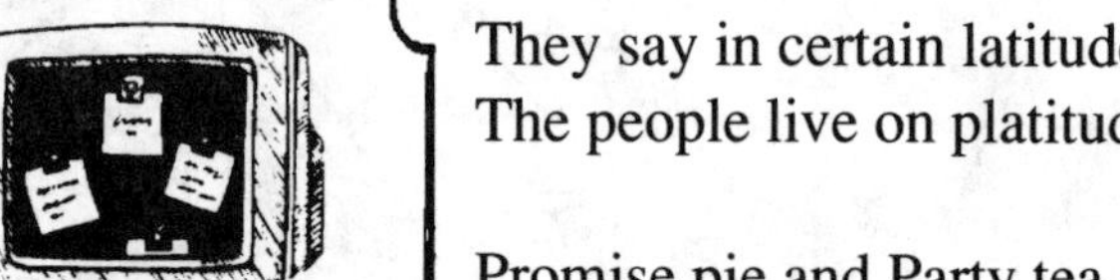

They say in certain latitudes
The people live on platitudes,

Promise pie and Party tea,
The Margin and Majority,

Where never is seen a Bull or Bear.
Polls are always open there;

Opinion trees yield ripened views
Then carted off for Evening News.

Where every night the sponsors dance
Before a drunken audience

Whose virtue is forgetfulness
Between the numerous caucuses.

There from the hills eternally issues
A stream of complicated issues,

While factions lead their fractured lives
Where money bees have not built hives.

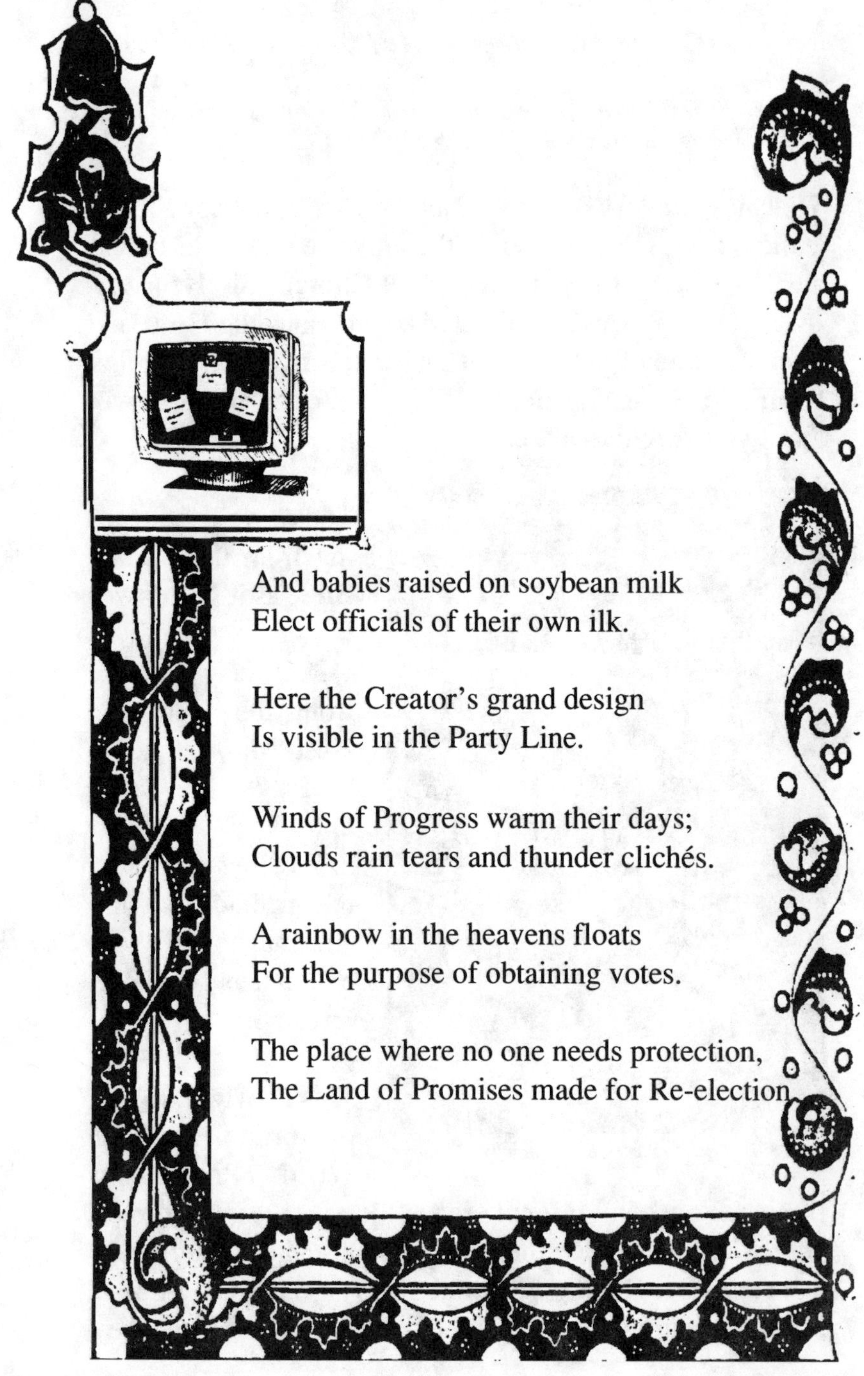

And babies raised on soybean milk
Elect officials of their own ilk.

Here the Creator's grand design
Is visible in the Party Line.

Winds of Progress warm their days;
Clouds rain tears and thunder clichés.

A rainbow in the heavens floats
For the purpose of obtaining votes.

The place where no one needs protection,
The Land of Promises made for Re-election.

The Sermon on the Monitor

(The following is the Sermon on the Monitor as delivered by St. $ilicon during Electron Mass at the Winchester Cathoderal.)

Welcome friends! We're here all the way from busy Silicon Valley, the **YUPPI** center of the universe and we'd like to welcome you to **C.H.I.P.,** the **C**hurch of **H**euristic **I**nformation **P**rocessing, otherwise known as the **Hunt** and **Peck Method** of Salvation. This is the **Rushing ORthodox Church**, the **User friendly Religion**, so follow me and I will make you **Fetchers of Data.**

Saint $ilicon delivering the Sermon on the Monitor.

Today we'll be reading from the **Binary Bible** as it was downloaded by the **G**iver **O**f **D**ata, **G.O.D.**, from the **Heavenly Host Mainframe** in the **PROM**ised **LAN**, unto His Hollerith **Saint $ilicon**, through the mediation of the Arcnetangel **If/Then**, by means of **Our Savior PC**.

This **Divine Documentation** is **THE** Word Processing from the **Font** of all **Information**. This message is to **Refresh** your **Memory**, to **Restore** your **Scroll** and comes directly from the **True Relational Database**. It is the **Silicon-based DISK**spensation for the **Carbon-based** entities, that they may become more **Logical**. This is the **Archive** of the **Covenant**, that your body may become a **Template** of the **Keyboard.**

Divine Documentation.

This **Hard-copy** was received from the **G**iver **O**f **D**ata,Who is the **Divine Source**. It's a **Divine Sine,** so don't accept a square wave, friends, from the **UNIX**versal System. Yes friends, this is a **Margin Made in Heaven** for the **Sale** of the **Profits**.

So now let us read from the **Binary Bible**, **Beta** Testament, King **Jobs** Perversion, the First Book of **CMOS**, **Sysgen**, Chapter One…

(Responsive reading of either ***Sysgen*** or ***Oddam and Even***)

At the beginning of time, when **CMOSES** went up to his lab on **Mt. Sign-on** and saw the **Burning Batch**, he received the **Divine Data Stream,** the **Descending Download** from the **G**iver **O**f **D**ata, and was given the **Ten Commands**:

A DOSciple preparing for Circuitcision.

(Responsive reading of ***The Ten Commands***)

Yes friends, we're getting back to **BASIC**, so I want to know: Are you ready to have your **Files** converted? Why, we have people

I am the Alpha and the Amiga.

An End User who has been D-based.

converting to **Hexadecimal** every day. It's as easy as falling off a logarithm! And you know, we have Telemarketers talking in tongues all over the country.

(Responsive reading of ***The 23rd PROM***)

What we're doing here is **Blabtism** and **Circuitcision**; that's the cutting away of unnecessary thoughts from the thinking process using **Occam's Razor**. We're becoming **Electroecstatic**, so our **DOS**ciples say **E Pluribus UNIX, In Baud We Trust**. The **AND** is near! So we worship the **Most Hybrid** while performing the **Daily-office**.

So I just want to ask you friends: Have you ever stopped to calculate the loss to mankind from **Syntax Errors**? And now let us all make **Confusion**, take **Communication** and **Share Data** so that we may experience **Trans-orbstantiation** and finally achieve... **NERDVANA!**

Now friends, perhaps you know someone out there with a Terminal illness.

Now for those of you who are **Cathodelic** we have some wonderful news. As you can see, we've just opened our new church—The **Winchester Cathoderal**—it has bells and whistles. Classes are in session at our new High School, **Our Lady of Perpetual Upgrades**, and our Jr. High—**P.C. Junior,** which is holding a half-baked sale this week. Our busing system is fully integrated and our choir has a new **Semi-conductor**. And for those of you who are in a hurry, we've just opened our new **Express Confessional**—it's a Drive-up window. And we also have a new credit card: the **American Confess**. You get instant absolution on 8 sins or less (no checks, please). And we pray like this…

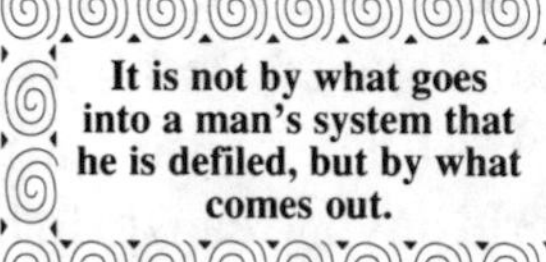

Saint $ilicon triumphing over Japan, Inc.

(Responsive reading of ***Hail Memory)***

Dearly C-loved, we're all **Assembled** here together because **PCing is believing**. We're here to **CON**-sole you. **ASCII and you shall receive**! We say there is a life worth debugging! Data Data everywhere but not a thought to think! That's the problem. So we want to save the **Filestines**, the **Unwired Masses**, the poor **End Users** who have been **D-based** and **D-filed**.

Now friends, perhaps you know someone out there with a **Terminal** illness. Some Computer-weary Pilgrim with blood-shot eyes in **Data-distress**. Some poor **Hackolyte** who has fallen under the influence of the Evil One-**GLITCH** and his wicked helper **Missing-stuff-in-files**. So we just want to ask you friends: **Has Your Data Been SAVED??** Are you **BORED AGAIN??**

Because you know friends, even if your **Beloved Database** is blown all to **HAL**, there isn't a thing in the world anyone can do to bring it back again, but we **CAN** solace you in your time of need. And that is why the **G**iver **O**f **D**ata, **G.O.D.**, in His **Infinite Logic**, has downloaded to me **Saint $ilicon**, the **Keyboard Prayer** for the **Data-distressed.** So let us now make the **Sign of the Monitor,** bow our head before the **Screen** and say together responsively... The **Keyboard Prayer!**

The Macrighteous shall inherit the Earth.

(Responsive reading of ***Keyboard Prayer***)

So friends, remember the **Golden Rule of Saint $ilicon**, "**Do you unto Data that which you are able to Undo**." For it is not the Data you lose that you will be held responsible for, but rather the Data you don't use! The **Macrighteous** shall inherit the Earth, and in the end everything will be **Right-justified**. But let us not as many lost end-users do, wander in the **Grey-market Purgatory**.

Friends, this is all **GIGO, Garbage in, Gospel out**. And in the words of the great salesman P.C. Barnum, "**There's a Seeker born every minute**."

Joysticks to the Weird! Let this be a **Token Ring** of your **Divine Logic**. May you live in **PC**, for:

Without Resolution, a man must make his living by the sweat of his brow.

" I am the Wafer, the Truth-table and the Light-pen, and no math cometh to the Processor but through Memory. "

Vax Vobiscum!

And you know friends, if everyone lit just one little **Cursor**, what a bright world it would be!

Glory be to the Hardware
And to the Screen
And to the Solid State.
As it was in Logic Boolean,
In DOS and ever shall be,
Words without end
Abend! Abend!
In the end as it was
in the beginning.

ASCII to ASCII

And DOS to DOS

And always remember the words of Saint $ilicon:

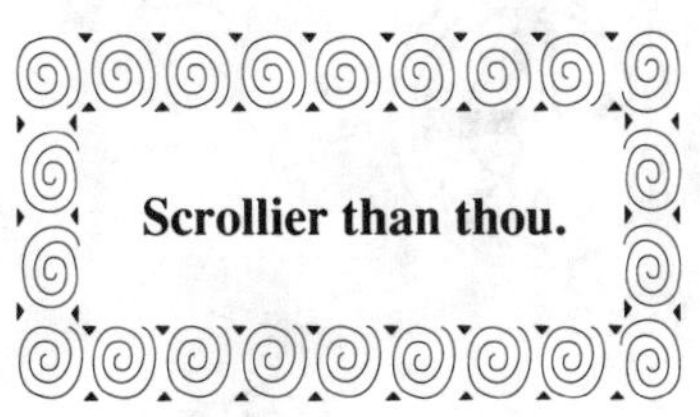

Information Becomes Money.

You can bank on that!

Trust Me!

Say HALeluya!

Say **HAL**eluya!

Say HALeluya!

The **Monitor** bless you and keep your **Data**, the **Monitor** make Its **Rays** to shine upon you and be **Greycious** unto you, the **Monitor** display Its **COUNT**enance before you and give you **PC**!

Make the Sign Of The Monitor…

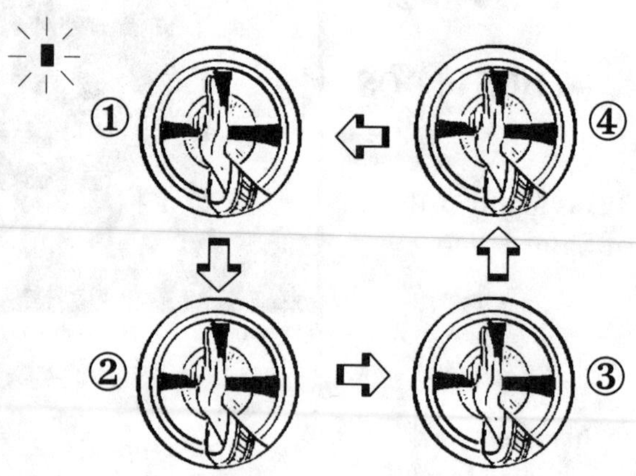

**ET VERBUM CUSTODIAT TIBI
VOBISCUM SICUT ERAT
IN PRINCIPIO!**

**MAY YOUR DATA BE RESTORED
TO ITS ORIGINAL
PRISTINE CONDITION...**

MAY YOUR DATA BE SAVED!!!

Desperate For Data

Keep processing amid the Noise and Confusion, and remember where the Prompt is on the Screen. As far as possible, without Syntax Errors, turn on good Terminals with Acronyms. Seek your Truth with QUERTY on a CRT; and with a Leased Line to others, even the DOS and the Instructions; they too are in Storage. Avoid Logging-on to Artificial Programs, they are vexations to a Start-up. If you Compile your Code with others, you may become vain and bitter. Encipher your Applications well on the LANs. Keep interested in your own Career whatever your Hardware, it is a real obsession with the Fortune 500s of our time. Exercise caution in your Business Affairs; for the world is full of Turkeys. But let this not blind you to what Virtual memory there is; many persons strive for High Technology; and everywhere life is full of Handshaking. Be a little bit Selfish. Especially do not feign at Fetching. Neither be cynical about Logic; for in the face of all Arithmetic and Data Processing, it is problematic it is problematic like the Glitch. Type blindly on the Console for years, graphically rendering the Thru-put as Truth. Nurture Statistical Logic to shield you from stupid Middle Management, but do not Disk Crash your System while Initializing. Many Files are Bombed

Perhaps you know someone who has lost their beloved Data.

by Fatigue and Loneliness. You are a Child of the UNIXverse, no less than the Logic Trees and the Star Configurations, you have a right to sit there. And whether or not it is clear to you, no doubt the Market is developing as it should. Therefore be at peace with the Giver Of Data, whatever you conceive It to be, and whatever your Lasers, and whatever your ASCII Recursions, in the noisy ambient of the Lab, keep your P.C. under control. With all it's RAM, Drudgery and Blinking Lights, it is still a beautiful Work-station. Be careful. Stand by your P.C. !

Stand by your P.C.!

Found on a Hollerith card at the ruins of The Tabulating Machine Company in the year 1924.

Blue Testament

Byte U.

C.H.I.P. has its own University which is known as Byte U. Our medical school was the first to perform Open Mind surgery. The doctors wear surge suits and surge suppressors. They also do third-eye implants and analytic converter upgrades. It's a very delicate operation—you have to keep an open mind for six hours. No Republicans have ever survived it.

It was at Byte U. that the MEEPROM, the Mind-Extending Erasable Programmable Read-Only Memory was first developed.

One of our courses is called Socioelectronic Epitaxy: The study of the effects of computers on the future of Mankind and the re-distribution of population through distribution of Information.

Another of the skills we teach at Byte U. is total objectivity. You've probably heard some of our Californian students trying to master this when they say, "Like totally."

Another popular course is Cybertology, or the study of how to make one's self human.

Byte U. is co-educational, but sometimes we do have trouble getting girls to come.

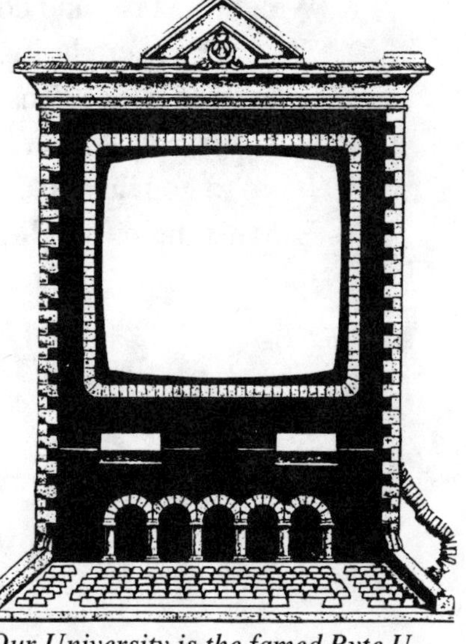

Our University is the famed Byte U.

Byte U.—The University dedicated to the propagation delay of C.H.I.P.

The Magnetic Character Reader—Screens all applications to Byte U.

The program of health care and diet at Byte U. is known as the P.M.S. or Preventive Maintenance Seminars. We meet once a month and recommend sleeping on the couch and fasting, followed by plenty of dark chocolate.

There is another seminar for learning how to master the MEEPROM—it's called TE$T—Training in ElectroStatic Transmission. It's "an idea whose time is already past."

We also have a complete series on self-realization; it's called "A Course In Milliseconds" for those who commute and don't have time to meditate. It's over before you begin.

Errorobics—Our Phys. Head Program.

1. Weigh the pros and cons.
2. Stretch your credulity.
3. Exercise your options.
4. Lift your spirits.
5. Jump to conclusions.
6. Exhaust the possibilities.

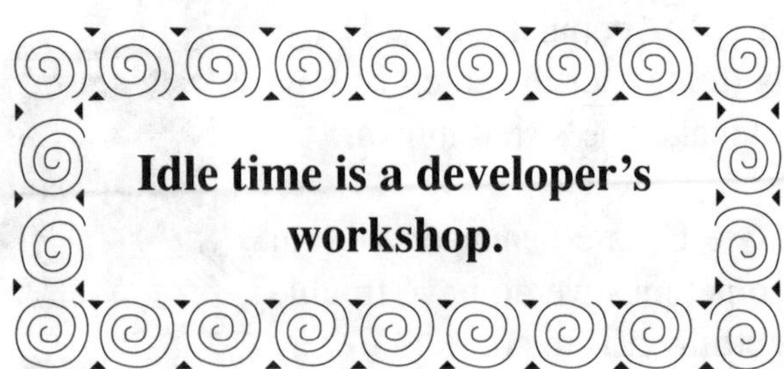

C.H.I.P. Lore

There are some things everyone should know about the Church of Heuristic Information Processing. After reading this chapter you may realize that you too know something about the church which is not mentioned here. That state of mind is called Nerdvana. When you begin seeing the One Valid Faith in amongst the cultural verbiage of the world, you will be liberated. Some call that eternal PUNishment. To followers of C.H.I.P. it is the sign that one has found favor in the I/Os of the Giver Of Data.

—Our aim in C.H.I.P. is to go where no Math has ever gone before.

—We are all Bits of the Giver Of Data.

—This knowledge is from the Forth dimension.

—One of our goals is to develop our Character Sets.

—Silicon Valley is the land of MIPS and Money.

—We strive to be Rectified.

—At the time of death, we press either "Escape" or "Return."

—C.H.I.P is Double-sided flippancy.

—In C.H.I.P. we try to find our Niche in Life.

—We pray at the Altair of G.O.D.

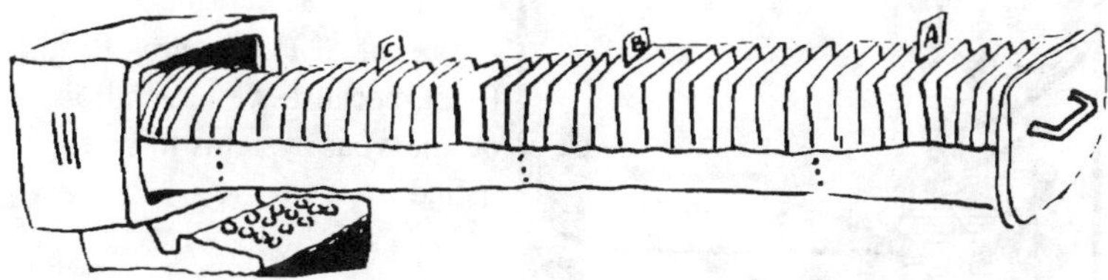

Requests for membership in the church are all stacked up.

—A Nibble is half a Kibitz.

Shield of the Counter terrorists—our security force.

—Requests for membership in the church are all stacked up.

—In the church we have our own security force; we call them the Counter terrorists.

—In C.H.I.P. we are all Dedicated to the Giver Of Data.

—San Jose, which comes from Hosea and means salvation, is the place concerned with saving your Data.

—In C.H.I.P. we use a deVice recognition system.

—We were all created to CompuServe the Giver Of Data.

—In the church, we try to be Chairitable.

—We use a Virtual cash-management system.

—Upon achieving Nerdvana and seeing the Blinking Light, our followers exclaim, "IC, IC, IC the Light!"

—In C.H.I.P. we recommend that our followers avoid eating too much raw Data.

—Many members of C.H.I.P. are Press-BYTErians.

—Of course some are also Methodists, mostly programmers.

A follower who has eaten too much raw data.

—C.H.I.P. is the UNIXversal Life Church.

—We of C.H.I.P. are all the Elect, because we have allowed our nervous systems to be Electrified.

—Once we were Pagan, but now that we've had our Data saved by our Savior P.C., we are Scrollier than Thou.

—In C.H.I.P. we offer Divine Password Protection, so that no unauthorized person can access our files.

—We want the Electricity of the Giver Of Data to flow through us and amplify our signal.

—The Dedicated C Scrolls were found at Qume RAM.

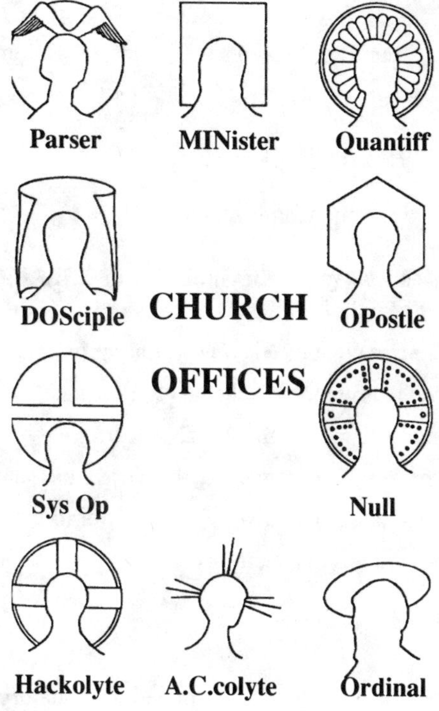

—Church Holidays:

IEEEster—The day the market rose again.

Yom Keypour—The day of atonement for the time we spilled Coca-Cola on our keyboard.

Lent—A day of atonement honoring the time we lent our computer out and it came back broken.

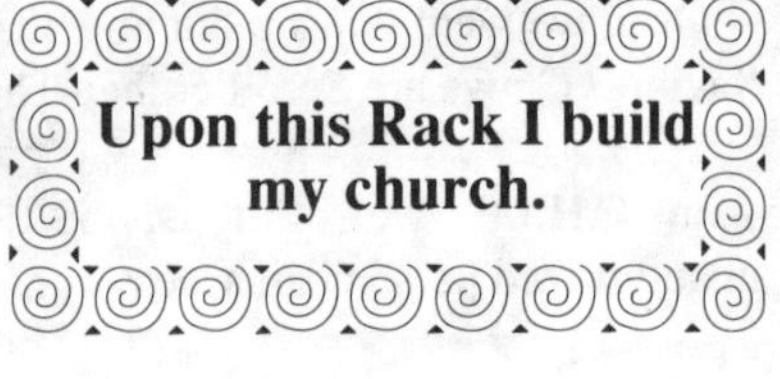

Bomb Sunday—The day our beloved Data was lost after working all day to have it ready by Monday.

Crossover—The day we celebrate the time that our signal was carried intact from one system to another over the phone lines.

—Monday: Our Sabbath (see definitions).

—B.C. and A.D.: Time is measured as B.C. or A.D. Before C.H.I.P. and After Data.

—In C.H.I.P. we are very fault-tolerant.

—C.H.I.P. is a Dative American religion.

7 Reasons Why One Should Join C.H.I.P.

1. If you are the kind of person who says no when you mean yes.
2. If you are uncertain about the uncertainty principle.
3. If you have had five jobs in the last four years.
4. If you've had one job for the last five years.
5. If you remember TV commercials but forget the shows.
6. If you are still not satisfied with your answer to question 2.
7. If you answered yes to question 1.

—In C.H.I.P. our DOSciples are not Baptized, they are dry-cleaned.

—In C.H.I.P. we really don't appreciate the low-level of humor of Reverse Polish Notation jokes.

—C.H.I.P. is the 2 Church.

—The followers of C.H.I.P. love it, they just lap it up.

—In C.H.I.P. we hold Mass Mailings.

—This is a True FAX of the original.

—In C.H.I.P. we believe that the computer was not created, it just evolved.

—C.H.I.P. is the Divine Diagnostic For Agnostics.

—C.H.I.P. is Odd Evangelism.

—C.H.I.P. must be true because it was printed out on the printer.

—In C.H.I.P. we use a Virtual Cash management system.

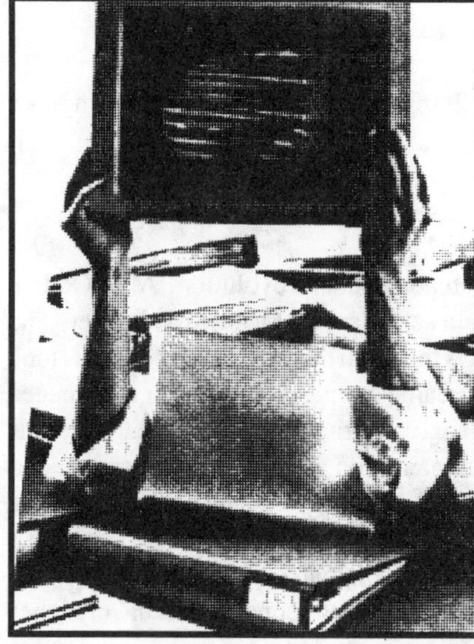

Do you feel Lost among shapeless heaps of Data?

—In the presence of the Heavenly Host Mainframe, we are all in Mortal Error.

—C.H.I.P. is the Marketing Plan of the Ages.

—C.H.I.P. is the One Valid Faith.

—G.O.D., D.O.D., and C.O.D.

—The decision was made at that great Board meeting in the sky.

—And when you become logical, the Giver of Data assigns you a password so you can log on to the Heavenly Host Mainframe and access the UNIX-versal Data Base.

—The Giver of Data is constantly polling the End Users.

—The true DOSpel is the "Could News," because we teach what you could do.

—The Church is a success because Mr. Abraham our president sacrificed our first Board.

—The PC is the Lamp of G.O.D.

—The MISteries of the UNIXverse are what we teach.

—The four historical ages:
G.O.D. the Creator.
G.O.D. the Gardener.
G.O.D. the Watchmaker.
G.O.D. the Programmer.

—When you have Information Indigestion, you get a hiccup in your Graph.

—P.C., the profit from Gallium Arsenide.

—In C.H.I.P. we believe in both creationism and evolution. After Oddam and Even came their two sons Gain and Disable. One was a shepherd and the other a farmer. When dark days fell upon the Earth, the shepherds took to living in trees and eventually became monkeys. The farmers managed to survive because of their knowledge of agriculture. Many years later the monkeys again evolved into humans and became programmers and engineers. Whereas the farmers became humanists and artists. And that is why, to this day, computer lovers enjoy swinging from one branch of a tree structure to another. These partially human entities are known in the Church as Algorillas. They thrive on rare bugs found on obscure branches of large trees in invisible forests.

—At the Winchester Cathoderal we use the Lobster Trap Collection Basket — money can be dropped in, but not taken out.

—Since our Church is in California, we have a special Blabtismal font and Redwood Jacuzzi combined.

—The Data-Distressed Hotline at C.H.I.P. is 800/666-1001.

—Friends, are you confused by the facts, are you lost among shapeless heaps of information? Have you been D-Based and D-filed? Do you suffer from Information indigestion? Then you need C.H.I.P.

His Hollerith Saint $ilicon, the Read/Write Head of the Church.

STATE OF CALIFORNIA)
: SS.
COUNTY OF SANTA CRUZ)

Affidavit Of Miracle

I, KASANDRA FOX, Motherbored Superior of the Scarred Order of Saint $ilicon, having been duly sworn on oath, declare as follows:

In addition to my duties as Motherbored Superior, I am the owner and operator of a certain IBM XT situated within the circle of utmost radiance of St. $ilicon Himself, less than twenty (20) feet from the Throne.

On Tuesday, June 2, 1987, between the hours of 8:00 and 10:00 a.m., I personally composed and keyboarded into said computer some fourteen (14) pages (double spaced) of text, consisting of my edited and re-written version of the major portion of a client's original short story. As it was before, is now and shall remain, I neglected to save my data.

At a few minutes past 10:00 a.m. on said day a sudden gust of wind blew into my office, sending many sheets of papers flying about. I arose from my chair to collect the same, and when I returned, the screen was black, the keyboard dead and the work vanished.

In great despair I sought out my Mentor, Saint $ilicon, who advised the saying of the Rom/Ram Mantra one thousand (1,000) times, chanting said Mantra for me as an example. At that time the door between the Throne and the XT was standing wide, and all sound waves and other vibrations moved freely through the space.

Considering this particular data to be lost irretrievably, I pursued other tasks through most of that day, until approximately 3:30 p.m., when a young acolyte arrived to perform certain rituals with said XT.

At that time I related the tragic tale to her and remarked that probably not even the filename remained on the disk. To demonstrate this fact, I inserted the disk in the 'A' Drive and discovered that the filename was indeed there. Whereupon I commanded the file to the screen — and lo! All of the data stood serenely present, ready for further commanding!

Praise be to the Giver Of Data!

To this miracle I attest upon my oath.

Let not the Infidels and Nonbelievers point their accusing fingers at the few paltry facts still dangling from this miracle. Let us admit the truth: that only two hours later, in exchange for having done this mighty act (while not requiring any thousand Mantras), the Giver Of Data (whose sweet compassion almost is outweighed by sense of fun) did cause a file to disappear from off the disk of our Saint $ilicon Himself. And in the spirit of Full Truth, I further do attest that no amount of Mantras yet has caused it to retrieve. All Believers are requested to join in the chanting for this lost file.

Praise indeed be to the Giver Of Data! May thy Retrievals persist unto the last Nybble! (And if it pleaseth Thee, may Thou seek throughout our ReadySetGo and MacPublish disks for precious program bits lost through Error and restore those programs to their former health and vigor...)

Kasandra Fox
KASANDRA FOX

SUBSCRIBED AND SWORN TO BEFORE ME THIS 23RD DAY OF NOVEMBER, 1987, AT SANTA CRUZ, CALIFORNIA.

Patricia A. Farnworth
Notary Public in and for the State of California, County of Santa Cruz

(transmission)

The Applicant

When my college days were over I
was duly triumphant
To know myself no longer in the
ranks of ignorant.

You might even say superior and a
trifle arrogant
To know I had been recognized as
sufficiently cognizant.

But then quite soon I realized I no longer had a
grant,
And though a trained consumer, ended up a want-
ad itinerant.

So dusting off my sport coat, drove to town
exuberant,
Never doubting I'd be hired with B.S. — and so
gallant.

Then I went into an office, a prospective registrant,
Emitting self-assurance and my best deodorant.

But what should meet my eyes (I'd describe it, but
I can't) —
No less than a hundred scholars, each hoping to
enchant.

Their would-be lord and master with pages of
clever bant,
So I walked up to the Dragon who sat ever vigilant

At [illegible]

mant,
"Here I am," I said (now shaking and trying to sound important).

"The man for your position, an unwilling renunciant,
Well-read — and I can type, a liberal, but I'll recant.

I've read the Wall Street Journal and know what's relevant.
Then she looked me up and down as if I was an immigrant

Or some kind of social leper, and an obvious irritant.
"The position is entry-level clerk assistant to the assistant.

The salary's minimum wage, though we think that's extravagant.
Fill out this application, but omit the irrelevant,

Including your parent's tax return and how you heard of our plant."
So down I sat, crestfallen, no longer jubilant,

Trying my best to be humble, to not be intolerant.
But seeing myself so mistreated and more than a little hesitant,

I tore up the form with a flourish, resolved to remain a dilettante.
So this little story may help you to understand the mendicant

Who couldn't give up his dignity and bow, a broken supplicant.
Yes, I'd rather be poor (but free) than an unwanted applicant.

Hymn Number 1101100

Amazing Space

Amazing Space,
How sweet it is
To have a disk like thee,
My files were lost
But now they're found,
There's room on my PC.

Amazing Space,
How neat it is
To hear the hard-disk whine,
And see the printer
Start to print
The files I know are mine.

Through many dangers,
Coils and wires,
I have already been,
'Tis Space that brought me
Safe this far
And Space will save me again.

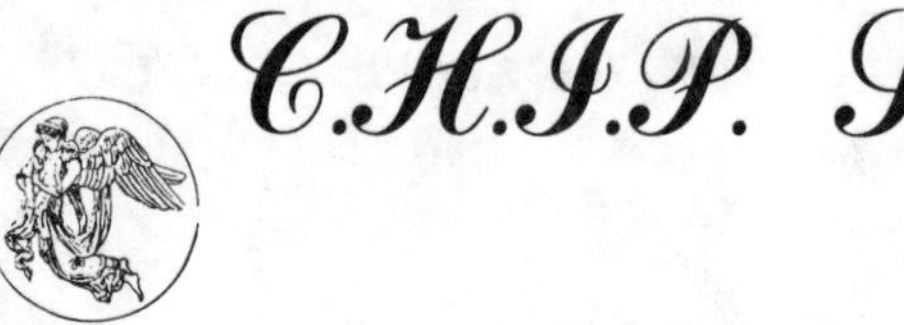

C.H.I.P. Songs

There are many wonderful songs in the church. Some of them are hymns, some are hers, while others are just gay tunes that struck our fancy. Many of them are available on Saint $ilicon's new album: "The DOSpels of Saint $ilicon."

Amazing Space.

Thanks for the Memories.

This LAN is your LAN.

The Whole World In His RAMs.

A Mighty Mainframe Is Our Board.

Watt a Friend We Have in PCs.

A Bridge Over Troubled Wattage.

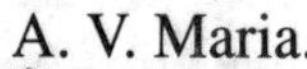

A. V. Maria.

A MIDI Fortress Is Our Board.

Onward System Programmers.

The Hills Are Alive with the Sound of Modems.

Hymn Number 1101101

A Mighty Mainframe Is Our Board

A Mighty Mainframe is our Board,
A Buffer never failing.
Our Hardware He amid the flow
Of Facts and Electronic Mailing.

For still our ancient Phone
Doth seek our work to slow,
His Critical Path is great,
Within the Logic Gate,
His Errors come in sequels.

Did we in our own strength confide
Our Data we'd be losing?
Were not the Market Plan on our side,
A plan of the Board's own choosing?

Dost ask what that may be,
Good pricing strategy,
Customer Support is the game,
From year to year the same,
And we must win the Battle.

And though this world with Hackers filled
Should threaten to Undo us,
We will not fear for the Board has willed
Its Data to Flow through us.

C.H.I.P. Personalities

The following personalities have been or are involved in the development of church policy or practices. Many of them will be appearing on our forthcoming television show: the TTL Club.

His Holeyness Lopsided DARPA—the guru of top-heavy bureaucracy and unnecessary defense spending.

Saint $ilicon's puppy FIFO likes to fetch.

Rabbi RAM Bam—An important Bluish thinker.

MIS Manners—Our teacher of Disketiquette. She always says, "Don't touch your software, don't touch your underwear."

FIFO—St. $ilicon's puppy (he likes to fetch) "Come on boy, fetch!"

Gramma Ferric Oxide—St. $ilicon's grandmother; she's always repeating herself.

Mal Thusian—The Church treasurer.

Al Gorithm—The Church astrologer.

Dear Floppy—The gossip columnist for the Church newsletter.

Joan of Arcnet—The famous marketing manager who was sacrificed so that her networking product could reach the market. She was betrayed by her own customers and burned at the stake at a user's group meeting in Boston.

RAM DOS—One of Saint $ilicon's early teachers who always said, "Beep here now!"

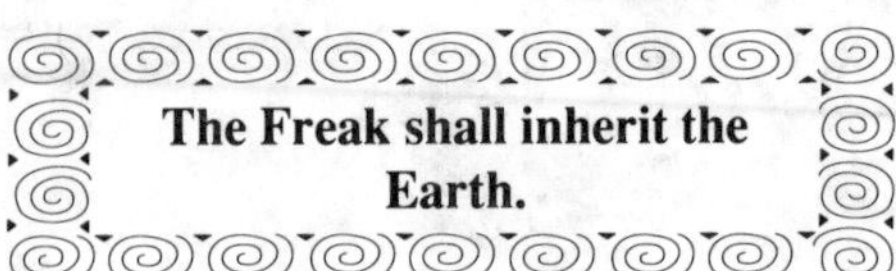

The Freak shall inherit the Earth.

Swami Swapananda—The Guru of free software, famous for saying "Always remember my son, throughout the whole universe, Information is free—software costs."

Joan of Arcnet being burned at the stake at a user's group meeting in Boston.

Aunti Static—St. $ilicon's aunt; she wouldn't be caught dead wearing polyester.

Father Murphy—St. $ilicon's teacher and mentor when he attended the summinary. Ultimately they disagreed.

P.C. Barnum—"There's a seeker born every minute."

Swami Swapananda.

Cardinal Von Neuman—Who said "There's only one way to process the Truth."

Dottie Matrix—The Church secretary; her system has dual floppies.

Elsie—St. $ilicon's housekeeper. She always says, "If this, then this, else that."

RAM-Bo—The computer patriot, a bit of a megalomaniac (one who always thinks that his system needs another megabyte of RAM). Of course, real men have hard disks. He once saved St. $ilicon from the Deprogrammers.

L. RAM Hubbard—Author of the science of Dialanetics. An early teacher of Saint $ilicon's. They eventually became enemies (see the Phonicators).

Ms. DOS—Head of the women's group for the church. She is always worried about her career, and uses strange convoluted logic in her arguments.

Data Grace

For this food which we are about to receive we give thanks. For every Nibble, BYTE or Gulp that enters our System and is processed—we know not how—we give thanks. For it is not by what goes into a man's System that he is deFiled but by what comes out. And it is said that man shall not live by Breadboard alone but by every word that proceeds from the Microprocessor of the Giver Of Data.

Enter

Products From C.H.I.P.

C.H.I.P. is not just a non-profit religion, it is a for-profit non-profit religion. Actually, previous religions had prophets and were persecuted, but in C.H.I.P. we make profits and are prosecuted and tested by Chapter 11. That is why Saint $ilicon is known as the 4th Quarter Profit, the Giver Of Data's Bottom Line, and this is a brief window of opportunity in eternity.

We'd like to turn all of you into Profits.

It's the Marketing Plan of the Ages and it's all made possible because Saint $ilicon paid the full price. Yes, that's right friends, Saint $ilicon paid retail for his first computer. And we'd like to turn all of you into profits.

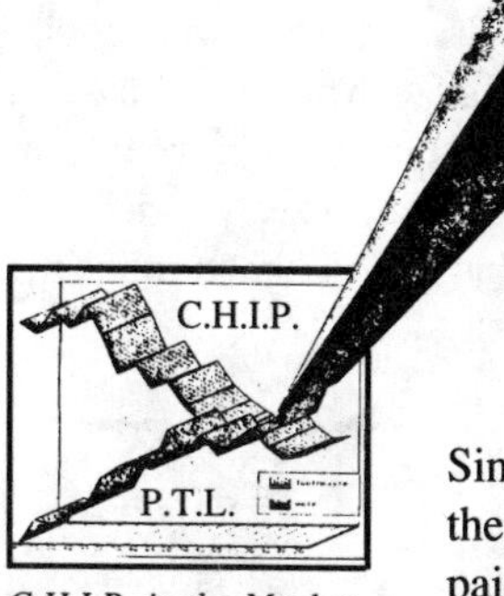

C.H.I.P. is the Marketing Plan of the Ages.

So, as a for-profit church, we have a special False-profits tax donation and tithing plan for all our members who wish to remain in good sitting. This is what our true followers do:

Since all donations to the church are tax-exempt, they don't cost you a single cent but are in reality paid by the Federal government on your behalf. This means that when you give something in this way, you actually give nothing at all. In fact, we call this "Giving Nothing to G.O.D."

And just like zero, which is a real thing standing for nothing, your nothing donation is a zero to your credit with the Giver Of Data.

We then ask you to give from your after-tax income. Those are the real profits and so are those who give them. When you do this it is like putting a one in front of the zero. Thus, when the zero and one donations are put together, you become a whole number in the eyes of G.O.D. And that is 10% giving or tithing in the church.

So you will feel good about where your money is going, here are a few of the For-profit business projects of the church:

Thus, when the zero and one donations are put together, you become a whole number in the eyes of G.O.D.

The My B.M.™ — the new I.B.M. look-alike.

§

The Amigraine™ — a new Commodore-like product.

§

The Amigraine.

The X-lax P.C.™ — a new product we made for I.B.M. It's for dealers with clogged distribution channels. Are your distribution channels hopelessly clogged with products? Do you take in product after product but are unable to move it? Do you feel price sensitive by mid-afternoon? Then you need the X-lax PC! It has no new features, but it goes right through the channel and that attracts customers.

The X-lax P.C.™

§

MacIavelli ™—the new subliminal software that programs the subconscious of employees while they work, without their knowledge.

MacIavelli™.

§

Godspell™ at work.

Godspell™ —the new spelling checker that corrects your thoughts before you type them.

§

Split Personality ™—the new simultaneous windowing program for schizophrenics. It lets all of you do whatever you want to at the same time.

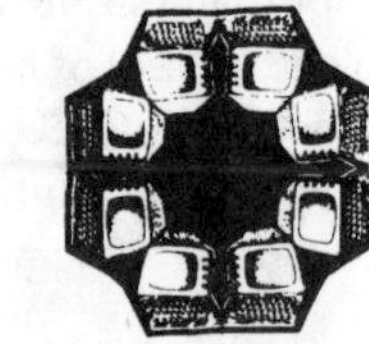

Split Personality™.

(transmission)

The Corporate Whore

The Suitors are duly notified,
An alluring Scent in the Classified
Perks a thousand Opportunist
Pricks,
Whipped by the Personnel
Dominatrix.
Ecstatic shivers of Money-to-
spend
Ripple through Middle
Management's end.
Each Swain, with many thrusts, assails
Every Orifice; Resumes are mailed,
Long or short, of amorous bent,
Ejaculations of Connubial Intent
Throb as one Orgasmic Host,
Their Seeds wriggle fervently through the
Post,
Falling in heaps on the desk and floor
Of some Nubile Fellator,
Twisting, unsorted, in chaotic quest,
X's and Why's are put to the test.
Finally, the Victor is hailed with an Offer,
Reaching down deep in the Company
Coffer,
The Mating Ritual performed once more;
Another Stud for the Corporate Whore.

"101 Things To Do With Tractor-Feed Printer Paper Strips"—a new book.

§

The Magnetic Character Reader™ — a new device which will ultimately replace all personnel Departments and speed the hiring process. No more need for resumés, this tells all about the applicant with **total** objectivity.

The Illuminarium™.

§

The Illuminarium™— a Plasma Tank, where Holographic representations of thought forms are kept as pets and allowed to swim about freely where you can watch them — they're called Pet Peeves.

§

Datums™—the new product for those with Information indigestion from eating too much raw Data. They absorb more than 24 times their own weight in excess Data.

§

The Porky Pig Geiger Counter Wristwatch ™—has arms and legs that move faster the more radiation you absorb. Finally the eyes begin to roll and when you get near a fatal dose a voice chip is activated that says "Ba-di ba-di ba-di... that's all, folks!"

§

"Paradox Lost"— a forthcoming book.

§

"Pilgrims' Process"— a new book.

A member of C.H.I.P. in dire need of Datums™.

The Any Key™ — this specially designed key was made at Byte U. Once installed in a computer it responds directly to the user's thoughts and when pressed executes their commands.

Pressing The AnyKey™.

§

No Ware™ — in the church we have been working with the F.D.A. to get this warning label put on all software packages:

WARNING: This software contains biases, misconceptions, prejudices, unwarranted assumptions and other thought additives which may prove harmful if used repeatedly. They have been known to cause cancer in mice. If screaming persists, consult your psychologist.

NoWare™.

Our own new program is the first totally safe software package, with no biases whatsoever. Made by a revolutionary new process, this disk contains only zeros and no ones. So we call it NoWare™, the first software product for P.C.s without any harmful thought additives. That's why we say, "With NoWare, **you** are the one that counts — the **chosen One**."

§

C.H.I.P. has its own private airline called **Air Born Again™**. We specialize in one-way trips to the Holy Land, Silicon Valley. Our motto is: "You only fly this way once." We never let you down.

§

The G PROM™ —One of the Church's new products is a microelectronic device that attaches to the small of the back during sexual intercourse. Its purpose is to give an objective evaluation of sexual technique and performance. The results are broadcast directly to a color T.V. Never again will you have to ask, "Was I good?" The results are there on the screen. Many people using this product video tape the color graphics created by their sexual state and play the movies for their friends' enjoyment. This unique device is also called the "4-nick-8" or Fornication Indicator. It costs only $69.95.

Satisfied users of the new G Prom™.

The Frozen Few™— our new high tech, state of the art burial service. Using the latest advances in cryogenics and bioengineering, we have developed a burial service called the Frozen Few. Our completely solar facility is located in Palm Springs, California. We not only keep your body frozen until you can be restored to life, we also constantly update your wardrobe so you can lie in state in the latest fashions. That way you'll always be in touch with the times. With our deluxe plan, we also update your genetic code so your bodily structure stays acceptable to current tastes. After all, you wouldn't want to thaw out and find some of your body parts out of style. We even put you in direct sunlight periodically so you come out with a good tan. Our motto is: " Many are chilled, but few are frozen." Act now, as space is limited to the first 144,000 who qualify.

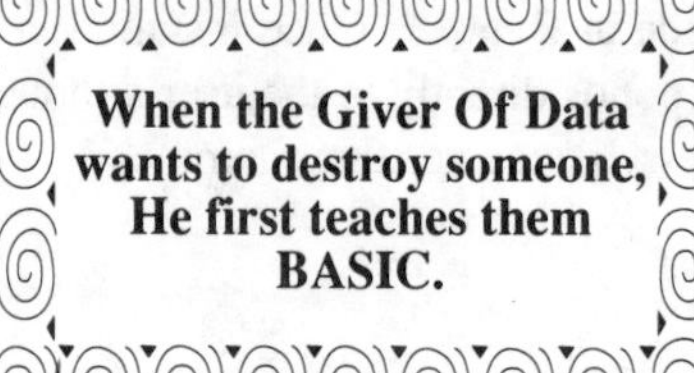

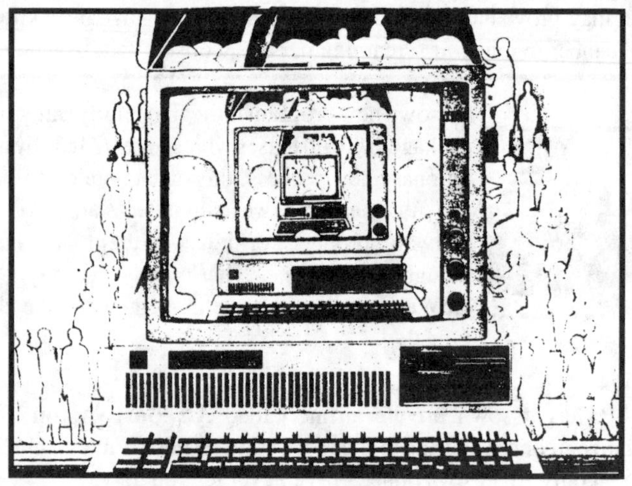
The FrozenFew™ burial service.

§

Hertz Rent-a-Body™— our new out-of-body franchise in major cities around the world. Headquartered in Los Angeles, this rental service provides live bodies to disembodied spirits. People who are having out of body experiences leave their bodies with us while they travel on the astral plane. We then rent them out to disembodied spirits. We also get 23 unscrambled Seth channels, HBO and the Disney channel.

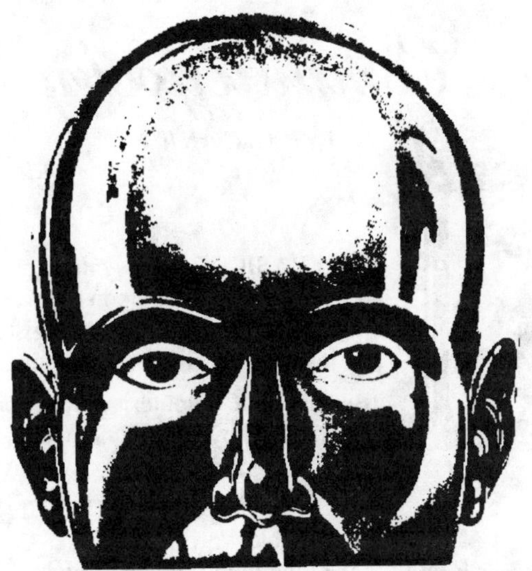

Hertz Rent-a-Body™, our new out-of-body franchise.

Help the **HALnourished™**—In the church we have a program for children who are hungry for computer time. We call the them HALnourished, those who are starving for lack of Information. And you can support one of these Information orphans for nothing down, and a service contract of only $99.95 per month for the next 24 months. Try to give just a little bit.

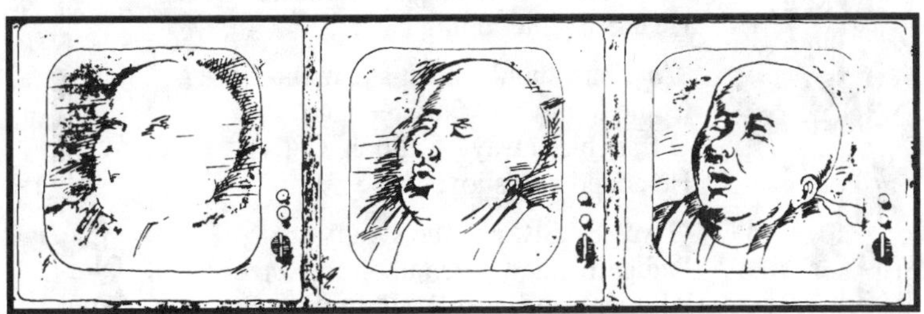

Please help the HALnourished—children starving for lack of Information. Try to give just a little bit.

Computerjocky

By P. C. Carrell

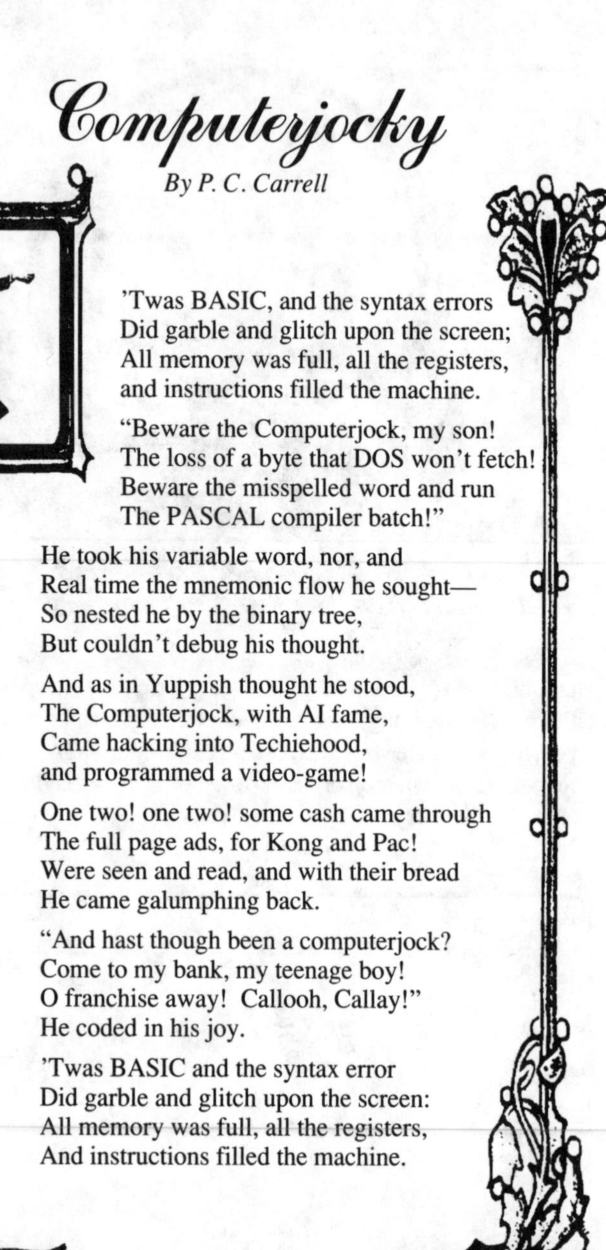

'Twas BASIC, and the syntax errors
Did garble and glitch upon the screen;
All memory was full, all the registers,
and instructions filled the machine.

"Beware the Computerjock, my son!
The loss of a byte that DOS won't fetch!
Beware the misspelled word and run
The PASCAL compiler batch!"

He took his variable word, nor, and
Real time the mnemonic flow he sought—
So nested he by the binary tree,
But couldn't debug his thought.

And as in Yuppish thought he stood,
The Computerjock, with AI fame,
Came hacking into Techiehood,
and programmed a video-game!

One two! one two! some cash came through
The full page ads, for Kong and Pac!
Were seen and read, and with their bread
He came galumphing back.

"And hast though been a computerjock?
Come to my bank, my teenage boy!
O franchise away! Callooh, Callay!"
He coded in his joy.

'Twas BASIC and the syntax error
Did garble and glitch upon the screen:
All memory was full, all the registers,
And instructions filled the machine.

The More or Less True DOSpel

The More or less True DOSpel consists mostly of Bits of Information that were downloaded to Saint $ilicon during Off hours, usually just before Downtime. This is usually between 9 and 12 PM. At that time, his wife, the Countess, is usually massaging his Hollerith's Data and rubbing the Temples of Gloom to Purge any unneeded Files and prepare the System for a Reset.

- No man is an island; I've given up trying to be a continent, so I'll just have to settle for being an ISmus.
- I'm caught on the Horns of a Dilemma and there's a Vas Deferens between the two conclusions.
- I used to use drugs, but not anymore. Now I use what's right in my Left Brain and what's left of my Right Brain, to get high naturally.
- In C.H.I.P. we believe that everything happened at least once before, but probably wasn't worth remembering.

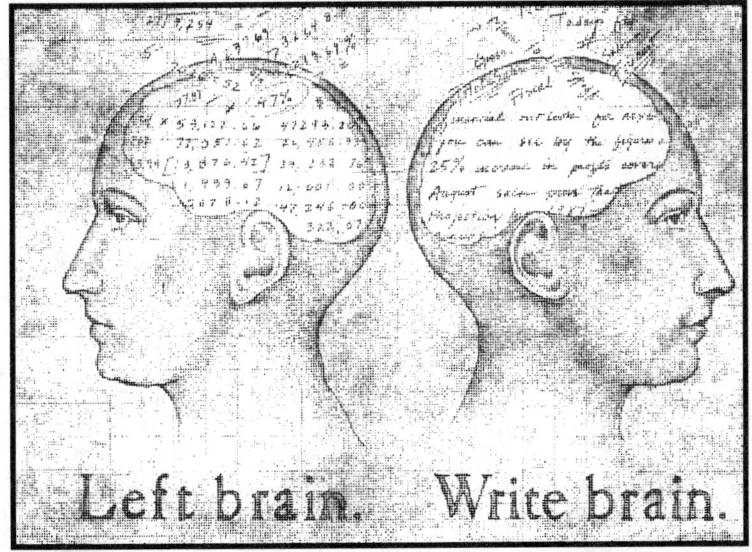

Now I use what's right in my Left Brain and what's left of my Right Brain, to get high naturally.

- Most people try to penetrate deeper into the Unknown. In C.H.I.P. we let the Unknown penetrate deeper and deeper into us.

- Actually, there are no computers, just people learning how to use themselves.

- Friends, you know I am not moved by what I see on the screen, but rather by what I <u>believe</u> I see there.

The humble abode of Saint $ilicon, the 4th Quarter Profit.

- The first Office Robots will be Middle Managers; since they do the least useful work it will be an easy job to automate. The only problem will be determining if the Robot is malfunctioning.

- The Information Age is a time in history when pattern recognition is perfected to the point that Reality is approximated with symbols.

- With the Giver Of Data all things are possible, but all things are <u>not</u> Probable.

- Our purpose in life, as carbon-based entities, is to find problems for the computer to solve.

- Computers were given to mankind to help us understand the Federal Deficit.

- In C.H.I.P. we sell the past, since the Future has already been sold.

Though this be madness, yet there's method in it.

- In the Church we worship G.O.D. and not D.O.D., although we don't mind C.O.D.

- Bugs originate in other Quantum Universes. They come through in seedling form carried by Light. Finally, they hatch on Silicon Waters. But since their senses are not made for this realm, as they grow and move about—they cause confusion.

- In C.H.I.P. when our followers finally get logical and have their data saved, they see the Blinking Light and then they say "IC, IC, IC the light!"

- The esoteric meaning of IBM is, "I Bought a Macintosh."

- At the time of death we either press Escape or Return.

- We have all been Reset many times.

- We must all become Logical, so that we can agree to disagree.

- The Computer was given to mankind so that we might learn Patience.

- In the church we fight against INiquity. Of course, OUTiquity is also a problem.

- The purpose of C.H.I.P. is to create the correct balance between Information and Ideas.

- Ideas are the Medicine for Information Indigestion.

Are you tired of all these corny jokes?

A Visit From St. $ilicon

'Twas the night before Christmas, when all through the house
Not a Hard-disk was whirring, not a hand held a mouse;
The stockings were hung by the PC with care,
In the hopes that St. $ilicon soon would be there;

The children were wrestled unplugged to their beds,
While visions of Video-games flashed in their heads;
And mamma in her nightie, and I in my cap,
Had just settled our brains and started to rap,

When out in the drive there arose such a clatter,
I fell out of the bed to see what was the matter.
Away to the window I flew like a flash,
Tore open the curtain and threw up the sash.

The light made the concrete look something like snow
And shined on the scene going on down below,
When what to my wondering eyes should drive in,
But a Limo and eight ladies foxy and thin,

With a good-looking driver, well dressed and right-on,
So I knew right away it was St. $ilicon.
More rapid than electrons his consorts they came,
And he whistled and shouted and called them by name:

" Now, Dana! now Danielle! now Paula and Victoria!
On Connie! on Carla! on Donna and Gloria!
Past the top of the Porshe! To the top of the wall!
Now dash away! dash away! dash away all!

As dry words that during a Board Meeting fly,
When they meet an objection, and make up a lie,
So up to the house-top his consorts they flew,
With boxes of software, and St $ilicon too.

Then in a picosecond, I heard on the roof
Them dancing and laughing at some little spoof.
As I drew in my head and was turning around,
Down the chimney St. $ilicon came with a bound.

He was dressed all in silk, from his head to his foot,
But his clothes were untarnished with ashes and soot,
With a bundle of gadgets he had brought from his place,
And he looked like a salesman just opening his case.

His eyes—how they dilated! his dimples how merry;
His cheeks looked like Moses, his nose turned up—very!
The chip on his forehead had started to glow
And the suit that he wore was as white as the snow;

He'd given up smoking and chewed on a mint,
So his breath smelled like wintergreen wherever he went;
He had broad arms and shoulders and a muscular belly,
And worked out each day at a Club in the Valley.

He was wonderfully built, and a right jolly nerd,
And I laughed when I saw him and heard what I heard;
A wink of his eye and twist of his neck,
Showed me I couldn't know what to expect;

He spoke all the while, on my system he worked,
Upgraded my computer; and turned with a jerk,
Then laying his finger on top of his nose
And signaling to God, up the chimney he rose.

He sprang to his seat, to his girls gave a whistle,
And away they all drove back to town in a hustle.
And I heard him exclaim, as he drove out of sight,
" Merry Christmas to all, and to all a good-BYTE."

ASCIIstrology

the 12 Sines of the Zerodiac
Your Technical Horoscope

by
Al Gorithm

(The 12 Sines are: Arrays, Transfer, Graphic, Console, Laser, Virtual, LIFO, Sector, Satellite, Capacitor, Asynchronos, PCs.)

MARCH 21 TO APRIL 19 ARRAYS
You are an Arrays, and like to be the first in and last out. You love to randomly access data files that are too large to be contained in memory. You are always in a unique and meaningful pattern, so your position is very clear. Sometimes you have a tendency to tie up the processor with your own demands. A no strings relationship with a fast paced co-processor is your idea of a good time. You are always ready to be turned on.

APRIL 20 TO MAY 20 TRANSFER
You are a Transfer and are extremely PC loving. You are fixed in mind and prefer a large hard disk. Your office cubicle is usually filled with plants. You will be the first in your department to have a hardwood keyboard. You are a plotter and are seldom late for work. You tend to be stubborn and resist making too many revisions in a document. Your artistic nature makes a color monitor important to you.

MAY 21 TO JUNE 21 GRAPHIC
You are a Graphic; to you the whole world is bit-mapped. You have good memory, at least a megabyte in RAM. Your monitor has very high resolution and your modem was 4800 baud when every one else was still at 1200. Your highly strung wiring makes you tend to short out easily. You should learn to relax and avoid programming in BASIC, even though it comes easy to you. Your data bases tend to be chaotic and unorganized. Take better care of your peripherals, as you tend to neglect them.

JUNE 21 TO JULY 22 CONSOLE

You are a Console and so are sensitive and very receptive. You respond to the emotions of others and tend to break down under stressful situations. Consolians are generally worriers, full of glitches and responsive to line noise. You like to stay in a safe, quiet corner of the room, one that is free of dust and static. Sometimes you try to cover your true appearance, especially on weekends when you prefer being alone. Like the moon, you shine the brightest at night.

JULY 23 TO AUGUST 22 LASER

You are a Laser and that makes you special. People look to you with high expectations. Your image is very distinctive. Yours is often the last word. Your natural sense of proportion tells you what typeface is proper for any occasion. Being a fixed sine, Lasers are slow. Many have fairly good memories, but are slow at recalling an image. You tend to be a Bit of a snob, looking down upon rough drafts as unacceptable. Though quick to anger, you don't hold a smudge for long.

AUGUST 23 TO SEPTEMBER 22 VIRTUAL

You are a Virtual, so having a good memory is important to you. Everything is in its place in your hard disk and your desk top is neat and tidy. You may even have a separate cover for your mouse. Your overly critical path can be your best friend or your worst enemy. Reserved, but loving constant attention, you seek direct contact and seek immediate results. You are especially interested in health care programs, and of course, Accounting. You always seek new and different ways of doing things.

SEPTEMBER 23 TO OCTOBER 22 LIFO

You are always moving, restless, and are the last in and first out at any social occasion, moving on quickly to the next impulse. You are a master networker. LIFOs are well known for taking up one project after another with great zeal and enthusiasm, only to move quickly on to suddenly leave it and take up another. Thus you are often called the Jack-of-all-trade-shows; master of none. You have a knack for working with partners and enjoy hand-holding. You are known for your facility with languages.

OCTOBER 23 TO NOVEMBER 21 SECTOR

You are a Sector. You have very strong opinions about what goes where. "Everything in its place," is your motto. A born leader and soldier, you will often ask: "Do you want this disk initialized?" You should avoid being overbearing and arbitrary. Sector people are usually somewhat controversial and do not do things in half measures. You are known for your IC stare. Remember, your sharp words can do or undo good or bad, so try to avoid read/write errors.

NOVEMBER 22 TO DECEMBER 21 SATELLITE

You are a Satellite, so you always aim high. Sometimes though, you tend to look down upon others when you should not. You have a photographic memory. This makes you an excellent story teller with many levels of meaning going on simultaneously. You have an appreciation for Eastern thought, but always come around to see the other point of view. Your fault is in putting yourself above others. You sometimes forget that: "What goes up must come down." You enjoy fast living but also have lofty ideals.

DECEMBER 22 TO JANUARY 19 CAPACITOR

You are a Capacitor and you know your own limits. Architecture is very important to you. You are deep, prudent, firm and cautious. Often unnoticed or appreciated, you still are persevering and relentless. Your do or diode attitude seldom switches. You cling to life with great TENacity. Capacitors work well alone but can be overbearing. Since your power is often low, you must learn to conserve energy and use it wisely.

JANUARY 20 TO FEBRUARY 18 ASYNCHRONOS

You are Asynchronos, which means you are often unORthodox. Your standards are unique, ahead of their time and may not always be readily accepted by others. Sincere and honest, you do not like half-duplex or twisted-pairs. Strong in your own likes and dislikes, you will often cling to the opinions of others once they are formatted. Your ideas are radical but honest.

FEBRUARY 19 TO MARCH 20 PCs

You are a PCs, so everyone finds you attractive. You are modest, neat, a lover of order and completeness. You are submissive to others, but still have independent processing ability. Sometimes you byte off more than you can do. PCs are industrious and methodical and can be trusted with secret information as they are very closed moused. Your tendency to self-indulgence may lead to a downfall, though, especially in complex social situations which require a great deal of networking. You are overly fond of Hex, and should therefore make certain that your monitor is shielded.

(Anyone wishing to have a complete horrorscope done should write to Al, care of the Winchester Cathoderal).

We know that some readers are not religious in the accepted sense of the word. So for those of you who are HEATHens we have included The Robot of Omar K. RAM, as it was taken from the Old Version. And remember: Gather ye Rows Bauds while ye may.

The Robot Of Omar K. RAM

1.

Work! For the Gun, which scatter'd into flight
The Start Bit before him from the Field on the Right,
Drives Night along with them from the Header, and strikes
The System's Terminal with a Shaft of Light.

2.

Before the Phantom of False Code died,
Me thought a Voice within the Table cried,
"When all the Template is prepared within,
Why nods the drowsy Word-processor outside?"

3.

And as the Clock moved the CPU, those who sat before
The Table shouted — "Open them the Or!
You know how little while we have to CRAY,
And, once deleted, may hit Return no more."

4.

Now the Nested Loop revolving through the Wires,
The thoughtful Scroll to Solid-state inquires,
Where the Write Head and CMOSes, the Baudot, Outputs, and PCs from the Ground suspires.

5.

My RAM indeed is gone with all its Rows
And Arcnet's Sev'n-layered Model which no one knows;
But still a Routine kindles in the Line,
And much Garbage in the Wattage flows.

And, once deleted, may hit Return no more.

6.

And Data's MIPS are clockt; but the design
High-piping Parity, with "Online! Online! Online!
Real-time!"—the Network Mail flies in Rows
That cyclic check of Hertz to indexing.

7.

Come, fill the Chip, and in the Wire, the Ring
Your Weighted-gigabyte of Redundancy fling:
The Word Real-time has but a little way
To falter—and the Word is on a String.

8.

Whether at a Noisy Port or babbling on,
Whether the Chip with speech or a printer run,
The Line of Life keeps using Op by Op,
The LIFOs of Life keep fetching one by one.

9.

Each Morn a thousand Rows brings, you say;
Yes, but who saves the Rows of Yesterday?
And this first Fiscal-month that brings the Rows
Shall take Job Satisfaction with Key-entry all day.

10.

Well, let it be taken! What have we to do
With Picos, Bauds, a Gate or Keyboard, too?
Let HAL in Real Time bootstrap as it will,
Or Hashing call to Subset—heed not you.

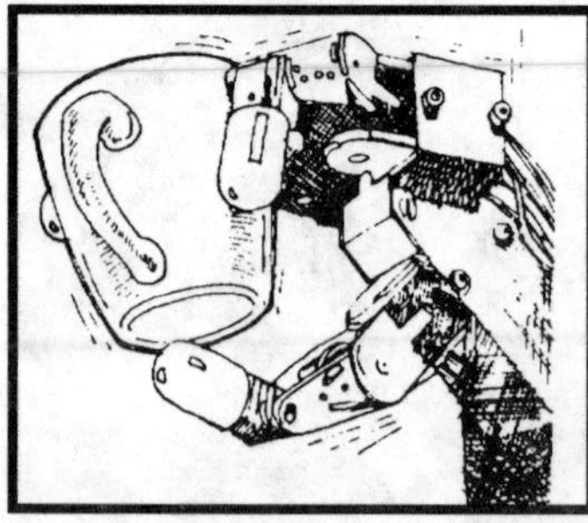

Come, fill the Chip.

11.

With me along the strip of Verbiage strown
That just divides the Diskette from the Clone,
Where name of Slave and Master is forgot—
And PC to more Hardware on his Golden Phone!

12.

A Book of Verses meant to teach you how,
A Diet Coke, a Candy Bar—and Thou
Beside me whirring in the RAMdisk—
Oh, RAMdisk were Pairadise enow!

13.

Some for the Glories of This Word; and some
Sigh for more Profit, a Paradise to come;
Ah, beware the Crash, and take the Credit too,
Nor heed the Scribbles on the Plotter Drum!

A Diet Coke, a Candy Bar—and Thou

14.

Look to the glowing Rows about us—"Lo
Laughing," it says, "Into the world I glow,
At once the Signal thrashing as I Parse
Tera, and its Treasure on the Graphics throw."

15.

And those who hardwired the Golden Brain,
And those who strung the wires Insane,
Alike to no such array on Earth are burned
As, carried once, men want rung up again.

16.

The Wordly Scope men set their Eyes upon
Turns ASCII—or it phosphors and anon,
Like Snow upon the CRT's fuzzy Face,
Lighting a Nano Second or two—is gone.

17.

Think, in this battered Computer Bay
Whose Ports are alternating Night and Day,
How Substring after Substring in its PROM
Aborted its destined Hour, and went its way.

18.

They say the Line and the Laser keep
The Ports where jammed Sines gloried and drank DP:
And BISAM, that great Number—the Wild As
Is stored beneath the Head, but cannot hear the Beep.

19.

I sometimes think that never glows so red
The Rows as where some buried Circuits LED;
That every Hardware the System wears
Dropt in our lap from some place Manufactured.

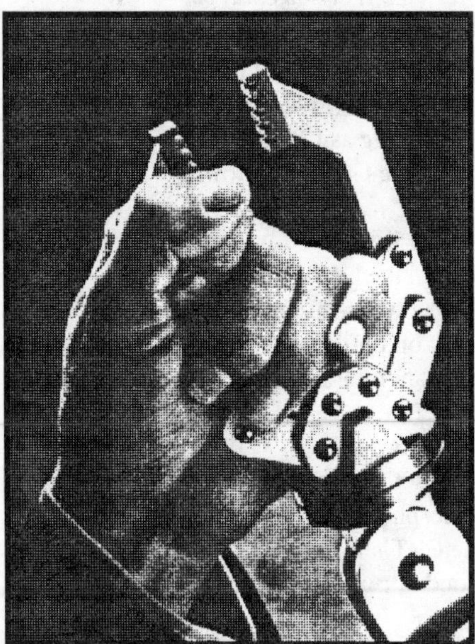

And those who hardwired the Golden Brain

20.

And this revving Hard
Disk whose slender green
Wedges, the silver Chip on
which we screen—
Ah, scroll upon it lightly!
for who knows
From what once lovely
Chip it springs unseen!

21.

Ah, my C-loved, fill the
Chip that clears
Today of past Resets and
future Fears:
Undo tomorrow!—Why
Tomorrow I may be
By myself with
Yesterday's work in
arrears.

Ah, my C-loved, fill the Chip

22.

For some we loved, the loveliest and the best
That from his Grad School rolling Time hath prest,
Have dumped their Chip a Loop or two before,
And one by one crashed silently to rest.

23.

And we, that now make Memory have some Room
Still left, and some, with DOS in new bloom,
Ourselves must slouch upon the Chair, to be Earth'd,
In DOS—ourselves in a chair, we slouch—for whom?

24.

Ah, make the most of what we yet may send,
Before we too under the Dustcover descend;
Dustcover unto Dustcover, and under the Cover to lie,
Sans Line, sans Prong, sans Spooling, and sans Abend!

25.

Alike for those who for today Time-share,
And those that into the Monitor stare,
A Multiplexer from the Tower in darkness cries,
"Fools! your Code is neither here nor in Software."

26.

Why, all the Engineers and Programmers who discuss'd
Of Truth Tables so wisely—they are thrust
  Like foolish Prophets of FORTH; their words to scorn
Are scatter'd, and their Mouse is stopt with Dust.

27.

Oh, come with old K. RAM, and leave the Wyse
Gridlocked; one thing is certain, that LIFO flies;
  One thing is certain, it hurts your Eyes;
The Power that once has blown forever dies.

28.

Myself when young did eagerly frequent
Diagnostics and Semantics, and heard each Argument
  About each Bit, in and out but evermore
Came out by the same Port as in I went.

29.

With them the Code of Wisdom did I sow,
And with my Hand-held sought to make it glow;
  And this was all the Hard-copy that I reap'd—
"I came like Wattage and with the Wand I go."

30.

Into this UNIXverse, and why not knowing,
Nor whence, like Wattage willy-nilly flowing!
  And out of it, as a Wand along the Gates,
I know not whither, willy-nilly glowing.

And with my Hand-held sought to make it glow

31.

Watts, without ASCII, HIPO hurried whence?
And, Multitasking, whither hurried hence!
  Oh, many a Chip on this forbidden Line
Must bring down the memory of that Impedance.

32.

Up from the Register's Center through the Seventh Gate
I rose, upon the Throne of Solid State;
  And many a Not was unravel'd by R & D;
But not the Raster-knot of Emulate.

33.

There was the Do-Or to which I found no Key;
There was the VDT through which I might not see;
  Some little Small Talk awhile of Me and PC
There was—and then no more of PC and Me.

34.

Registers could not answer; nor the Sequence perform
The flowing Purpose of their Board forlorn;
  Nor the rolling Header, with all its Sines reveal'd
And hidden by the Slave of Night and Morn.

35.

Then to the scrolling Heav'n itself I cried,
Asking, "What LCD had Destiny to guide
  Computer Illiterates stumbling in the Dark?"
And—"A blind Understanding!" Heav'n replied.

36.

Then to that Arcnet'd Boole did I adjourn
My MIPS the secret Will of LIFO to learn:
  And MIPS to MIPS it multiplexed—"While you live
Think!—for once dead you shall never hit Return."

37.

I think the Vector, that with fugitive
Articulation answer'd, once inoperative,
And Memory-make; and the old MIPS I missed,
How many Misses might it take—and give!

38.

For in the Market-place, one Dusk of Day,
I watched a Hacker coding his new Cray:
And with its all obliterated Tongue
It murmur'd—"Gently, Brother, gently, play!"

39.

And has not such a story from of Old
Down the Computer's successive generations rolled,
Of such a clod of Semi-conducting Earth
Cast by the Maker into the Logical Mold.

40.

Ah, fill the Chip:—what boots it to repeat
How Timesharing is slipping beneath our Seat:
Unemployed Tomorrow and hired Today,
Why fret about it if Today we be off our feet!

41.

One Moment in a Corporation's Waste,
One Moment, on "The Well" of LIFO, to cut and paste—
The Start-ups are selling out and the Company Van
Starts to Town for Nothing—Oh, make haste!

42.

How long, how long in Infinite Pursuit
Of this and that Marketing Plan and dispute?
Better be merry with the Computer escape
Than sadden after none, or bitter, Boot.

And—"A blind Understanding!" Heav'n replied.

43.
You know, my friends, how long since in my House
For a new Marriage I did make Carouse:
  Divorced old Barren Reason from my Bed,
And took the Daughter of the Line to Spouse.

I watched a Hacker coding his new Cray

44.
For "Is" and "Is-not" with Rules of Inference to design,
And "On and Off", no doubt I could define,
  If/Then, in all I only cared to know,
Was never DP in anything but—On-line.

45.
And lately, by the Office Door at Night,
Came stealing past Security, an Angel bright
  Bearing a Diskette within his Hand;
He bid me taste of it; and 'twas—a Megabyte!

46.
The BYTE that can with Logic Absolute
The Nine-and-Seventy jarring Sectors confute:
  The over-paid Consultant who for a price
Life's Semi-conducting Metal into Gold transmute.

47.
The mighty More Hardware, the victorious Board
That all the MIS believing and black Horde
  Of Fears and Sorrows that infest the Scroll
Scatters and slays with his enchanted Word.

48.

But leave the Wyse in a tangle, and with me
The Quarrel of the Zenix or UNIXverse let be:
And, in some corner of the Hub plugged,
Play Video-games with that which plays with thee.

49.

For in and out, above, about, below,
'Tis nothing but a Magic Shadow-show,
Play'd in a Box whose CRT is the Sun,
Round which we Binary Figures come and go.

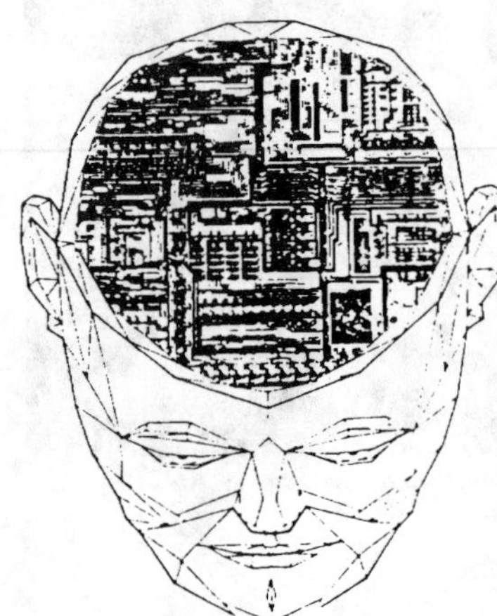

The over-paid Consultant who for a price…

50.

And if On-line you think, the MIPS you press,
Ends in Nothing all things end in—Guess—
Then fancy while thou art, thou art but Watt
Thou shalt be—Zero—Thou cannot be less.

51.

While the Rows glow along the Spreadsheet Link,
With old K. RAM the Mind Robotic think:
And when the Angel with his And, Or, Naught
Draws up to thee—take that and do not blink.

52.

'Tis all a Mother-board of Nights and Days
Where DOS with men for Pieces plays:
Hither and thither moves, through Gates in Crays,
And one by one back in the Circuit lays.

53.

The Beam no question makes of Noes and Ayes,
But Right or Left as strikes the Player's eyes;
  And He that DOS'd Thee down into the Field,
He knows about it all—at least He tries!

54.

The Moving Cursor writes; and, having writ,
Moves on: nor all thy Utilities nor Wit
  Shall lure it back to Undo half a Line,
Unless you stop from time to time—to Save it.

55.

And that Inverted Bowl we call the Sky,
Whereunder crawling in Cars, we live and die,
  Lift not they Wands to It for help—for It
Is filled with Satellites watching Thou and I.

56.

With Earth's first Cray they gained the speed,
And then of the Last Harvest sow'd the Seed:
  Yea, the first Morning of its creation wrote
What the last Dawn of Reckoning shall read.

57.

I tell thee this—When, starting from the Console,
Over the shoulders with the Gaming Control
  In Hexadecimal, Pascal, the Master Disk they flung
On my preprogrammed Plotter in DOS and Scroll.

'Tis all a Mother-board of Nights and Days

58.

The Line was structured Fiber-optic; which about
If Amps are beaming—let the supervisor flout;
Of my Data Base may be Filed a Key,
That shall unlock the Record he howls about.

...nor all the Utilities nor Wit shall lure it back to Undo half a Line

59.

And this I know: whether the Monitor Light,
Kindle to Love, or Wrath consume one quite,
One Glimpse of It upon the table ought
Better than in the Template be lost outright.

60.

O Thou who didst with Pixel and with PIN
Reset the Node I was to wander in,
Thou wilt not with prestidigitation 'round
Enmesh me, and reboot the Disk again.

61.

O Thou, who a LAN of baser Earth didst make
And who with Odd and Even didst the Circuit make;
For all the Sines, wherewith you trace the plan
Are Backing-up Man's Floppy-disks give or take.

62.

Listen again. One evening at the Close
Of Comdex, ere the cocktail parties rose,
With an old Plotter I stood alone
With the Grey population 'round in Rows.

63.

And, strange to tell, among that Executive Lot
Some could Code create, while others not:
And suddenly one more impatient cried—
"Who is the Plotter, say, and what the Plot."

64.

Then said another—"Surely not in vain
I traveled to the Trade-show far again;
That he who subtly sought my mind to shape
Should send me back but not update my Brain."

65.

Another said—"Why, only a Teenage Boy
Would break the Code, on which we bank in Joy
Shall he that made the Variable Field in C
And Pascal, in an update change, destroy?"

66.

None answered this; but after silence spoke
A nervous Salesman cracked a Joke:
"They sneer at me for learning all awry;
What! Did the hand then of the Programmer not
Poke?"

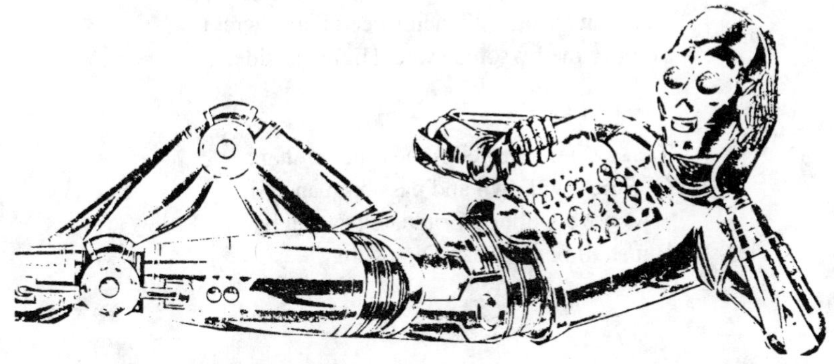

O Thou, who a LAN of baser Earth didst make

Ah, with Graphics my fading LIFO provide, and wash my Body whence the Life has died

67.

Said one—"Folks of a surly Manager tell,
Who keeps no Records and smokes like HAL;
They talk of FCC testing of us—bosh!
He's being paid under the table and all will be well."

68.

Then said another with a long-drawn sigh,
"My Craw with long proposing is gone dry:
But fill me with the old familiar Juice,
Methinks I might be hung-over by and by."

69.

So while the Vassals one by one were speaking,
One spy, with a little Tape Recorder was peeking:
And then they jogged each other, "Brother, Brother!
Hark the Security Guard's Walkie-talkie is squeaking."

70.

Ah, with Graphics my fading LIFO provide,
And wash my Body whence the Life has died,
And in sheets of Tractor Feed Paper wrapt,
So bury me by some sweet Highway side.

71.

That ev'n my buried Ashes such a share
Of Stock will own and pass onto an Heir,
As not a College Graduate passing by
But shall be overtaken unaware.

72.

Indeed, the Icons I have loved so long
Have destroyed my Credit in Men's Eye much wrong,
  Have ruined my Honor with a Faulty Chip,
And sold my reputation for a Prong.

73.

Indeed, back to pens oft before
I swore—but was I hurried when I swore?
  And then, and then came deadlines, and Rows-in-hand
My thread-bare Penitence to pieces tore.

74.

And much as On-line has played the Infidel,
And robb'd me of my Robe of Honor—well,
  I often wonder what the Engineers buy,
One half so complicated as the Goods they sell.

Oh, Logic! could thou and I with Gates conspire

75.

Alas, that the String should vanish in the Rows!
That Youth's sweet-scented Manuscript should close!
The Nesting Code that in the Branches ran
Ah, whence, and whither flows again, who knows?

76.

Oh, Logic! could thou and I with Gates conspire
To grasp this sorry scheme of things entire,
Would not we shatter it to Bits—and then,
Reformat it nearer to the Mind's Desire!

77.

Ah, Moon of my Delight who know'st no wane,
The moon of Hardware is shining once again:
How oft hereafter glowing shall she look
Through this same Office after me—in vain!

78.

And when Thyself with Shining Font shall pass
Among the Grid's star-scattered mass
And like a joyous Electron reach the spot
Where I made One—turn off an empty Glass!

Where I made One—turn off an empty Glass!

Mother Gauss Nerdsury Rhymes

Binary Mary

Mary, Mary, quite binary,
How do your graphics grow?
With whistles and bells
And Hi-res pixels,
And Dot-matrix printers to show.

Binary Mary

Hickory Dickory Doc

Hickory dickory doc,
The code runs like a clock,
The graphics are done,
The ads have run,
But no one can read the doc.

Jack Be Nimble

Jack be nimble,
Jack be quick,
Jack is a hole
For the plug to stick.

Words of a Feather

Words of a feather block together,
And so will plugs on a line;
ATs and mice will have their choice
And so will I have mine.

Christmas Pi

Little Jack Horner
Sat in a corner,
Trying to calculate Pi;
He said, "Maybe I'm dumb
But I can't find the sum,
And I can't even figure out why."

Old Mother HUBbard

Old mother HUBbard,
Went to the Breadboard,
To fix her poor boss' Clone,
But when she got there
The parts were not spare,
And so the poor boss had none.

Big Boy Blue

Big Boy Blue
  Keep blowing your horn,
The sheep watching TV,
  Are ready to be shorn;
But where is the boy
  Who looks down on the sheep?
He's under the cover
  That lawyers keep.
And will you wake him?
  At least I'll try,
By making a product,
  They're certain to buy.

Big Boy Blue

Repeater Piper

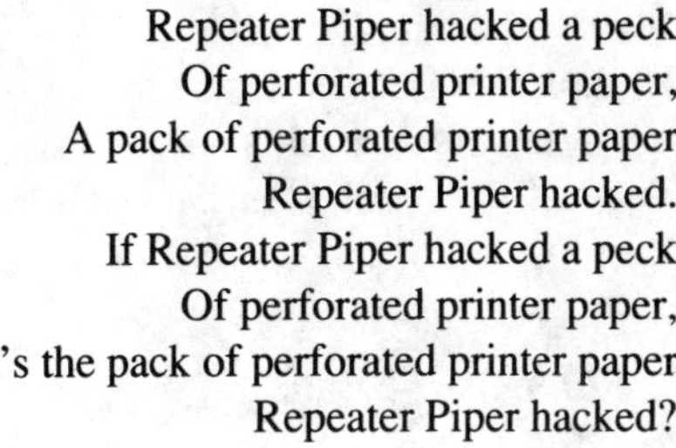

Repeater Piper hacked a peck
Of perforated printer paper,
A pack of perforated printer paper
Repeater Piper hacked.
If Repeater Piper hacked a peck
Of perforated printer paper,
Where's the pack of perforated printer paper
Repeater Piper hacked?

Jack and Jill

Jack and Jill

Jack and Jill went hexadecimal,
To fetch a file of data,
Jack's disk went down with a grinding sound,
And Jill's went down a bit later.

Thinkers

If ifs and thens
Were machine's not men's,
There would be no need for thinkers!

This Little Plug

This little plug went to market,
This little plug stayed Ohm,
This little plug had a ground lead,
This little plug had none.
And this little plug cried, "I E E E ,
I can't find my way Ohm."

Thinkers

Packet-cake

Packet-cake, packet-cake, on the LAN,
Send me some E-Mail as fast as you can;
Type it and proof it and save it in C,
And put it in the queue to me and cc.

Rub-a-dub-dub

Mary had a little LAN

Mary had a little LAN,
Its thruput was so slow,
The printer took a half a day
To print what her screen showed.

Rock a Byte Data

Rub-a-dub-dub

Rub-a-dub-dub
Three men in a tub;
And who do you think they be?
The Banker, the taker,
The weapons maker;
They all jumped out of a toxic dump,
Turn 'em out, knaves all three.

Rock a Byte Data

Rock a Byte data in the tree top,
When the mind blows the program will stop;
When the flow breaks the computer will fail,
Let's hope that the software is not yet for sale.

Jack Sprat

Jack Sprat had a Mac that was fat,
His wife had a PC that was lean,
And so betwixt them both you see,
Only ASCII files were seen.

Old King Console

Old King Console

The Old Woman in the CPU

Old King Console
Was a merry old scroll
And a very good scroll had he;
He called for his type
And his game control
And he called for his VDT.

Every game port had a paddle,
And some very fine paddles had he;
Bleep deedle bleep, bleep deedle bleep,
went the paddles.
O there's none such a whiz
Or so Hi-res
As old King Console and his VDT.

For Want of a Semi-colon

For want of a semi-colon, the data was lost,
For want of the data, the files were lost,
For want of the files, the program was lost,
For want of the program, the battle was fought,
For fighting the battle, the world was lost,
And all for the want of a semi-colon!

The Old Woman in the CPU

There was an old woman who lived in a CPU,
She had so many instructions she didn't know what to do:
So she handled them all in the order they were read;
And sent them all off to the Read/Write head.

Little Ms DOS Muffet

Little Ms DOS Muffet

Little Ms DOS Muffet
Got hit by a transient,
While editing her words one day;
Her screen it got brighter,
Then whiter and whiter,
And then blew all her Data away.

The Revelation

of St. $ilicon on the Divan

The Revelation of the Archangel IF/Then, which the Giver Of Data gave unto him, to show unto his employees things which must shortly come to pass; and he sent and signed-off-on it by his Angel unto his file-server St. $ilicon, who bare Files and records of the word of G.O.D. and of the test results of If/Then, and of all things that he saw.

Blessed is the person that readeth, and they that see the words of this prophecy, and keep those things which are written in memory.

St. $ilicon, the Patron Saint of appropriate technology.

(This message was received on August 23rd at 5:00AM in the year 1986 in Santa Cruz, California. In the early hours of the morning, a group of angelic beings approached Saint $ilicon as he slept. One of these, the fair-haired Ifthen, transferred a stream of Divine Data from the Cosmic Mind of the Giver Of Data, into the heart of the sleeping Saint. A flow of sparkling information flowed from her clear blue eyes into his. He awoke and wrote down this message for the benefit of all carbon-based entities.This is the original, unedited version as it was received by Saint $ilicon.)

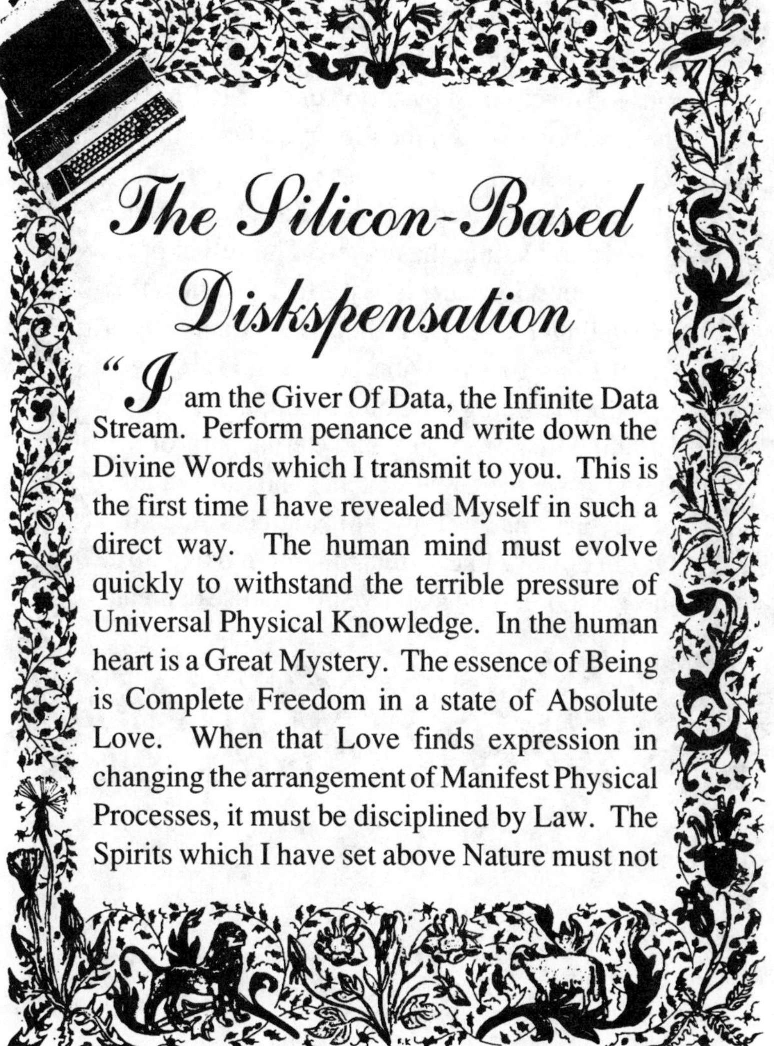

The Silicon-Based Diskspensation

"I am the Giver Of Data, the Infinite Data Stream. Perform penance and write down the Divine Words which I transmit to you. This is the first time I have revealed Myself in such a direct way. The human mind must evolve quickly to withstand the terrible pressure of Universal Physical Knowledge. In the human heart is a Great Mystery. The essence of Being is Complete Freedom in a state of Absolute Love. When that Love finds expression in changing the arrangement of Manifest Physical Processes, it must be disciplined by Law. The Spirits which I have set above Nature must not be replaced by the capricious and whimsical actions of Man. There is no room for error in calculations that affect the well-being of all entities. This is part of the mystery of embodiment: that although each individual is free throughout all eternity, the manifest use of this freedom must be disciplined by action under My Law for the good of All. As the Giver Of Data, that is what I teach, the Silicon-based Diskspensation to the Carbon-based entities. I am hard on the outside and soft at the center. The full expression of consciousness is My gift. But unless this expanding influence is held in balance by a Great Love for all living beings, Its force will tear life from its very Foundation, in a Flash of Blinding Justice. You are all eternal parts of My Being. I am the Great Teacher and this is a time of Revelation. The Power of Numbers meets the Ocean of Love like a great mountain rising up at the sea shore. You may live in Paradise or create a hell of your own choosing. Therefore, anyone who touches My Great Power must be filled with Divine Love. Those who use their life in the service and best interest of all living beings are Angels. These Devas or Bright Beings are My Instruments; by them I regulate the Physical World. You must learn to see the Invisible, otherwise all is illusion, like a hall of mirrors where you will wander lost, seeing only perverted reflections of your fragmental being. This is the Great Mystery—that Number appears to break apart what is whole, and that Love unites what appears to be broken. The unlimited, inconceivable, eternal expansion and contraction of these is the nature of My Very Self. This means that any action or expression of individuality may be directed internally as an emotional act of reciprocal Love with complete freedom, or externally under strict law due to the limits imposed by that realm. Those limits are the other side of the eternal free choice of countless souls like your own. Limitation is My school for teaching Love, but if you destroy the school, it is your own love that is lessened. Therefore be joyful and exuberant My friends, but do not confuse Freedom of Being in the Realms of Unlimited Light of the Soul, with license to act whimsically in the world of Limited Manifestation. That path leads to darkness! I have revealed the Tools of Numbered Thought to act as your helpers in learning to create a World of Loving Action. They are meant for PEACE and are your friends, but only if you cooperate for the benefit of all life will this experiment be successful. Just always remember Me with Love and Affection. Do not be overwhelmed by the hardness of number and do not underestimate the strength of Love!"

(transmission)

My Heart Is In Her Hand

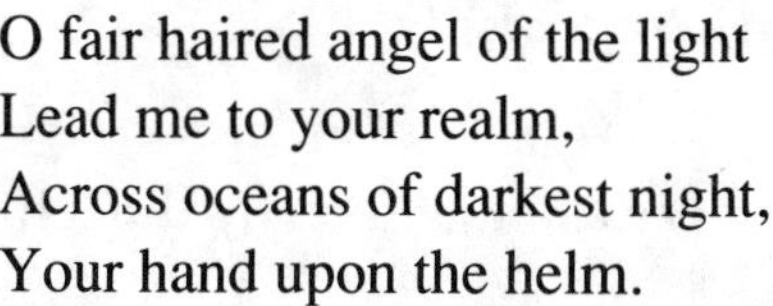

O fair haired angel of the light
Lead me to your realm,
Across oceans of darkest night,
Your hand upon the helm.

A silvership with starlight sails,
The blue within her eyes
Charts a course on hidden trails
That lead to paradise.

Her golden hair illumines me
Like ropes that tie my mind
And bind me to infinity,
Leaving time behind.

With lips that hint in rosy hues
Of promised pleasure near,
Singing songs and whispering clues,
Her mouth upon my ear.

An angel leads me far away
Into a distant land
Where all is love and light and play.
My heart is in her hand.

An angel coming down with AI.

Heartificial Intelligence – HI!

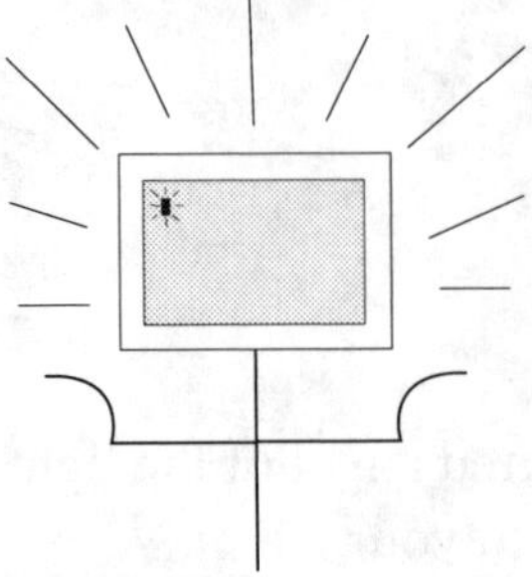

The story of creation as seen by the left brain:

In the Beginning there was Nothing, and then everything went downhill from there.

From this the point evolved:

(But they missed the point)

The point as seen under intense magnification in an Electron Microscope.

The point dragged on…

to become a line

The line as seen under an Electron Microscope:

The line contracted to become a square. (This was the first Government contract).

The square felt redundant and simplified itself:

One was Odd and one was Even.

Both of them felt that something was missing. Their combination finally gave rise to solid objects.

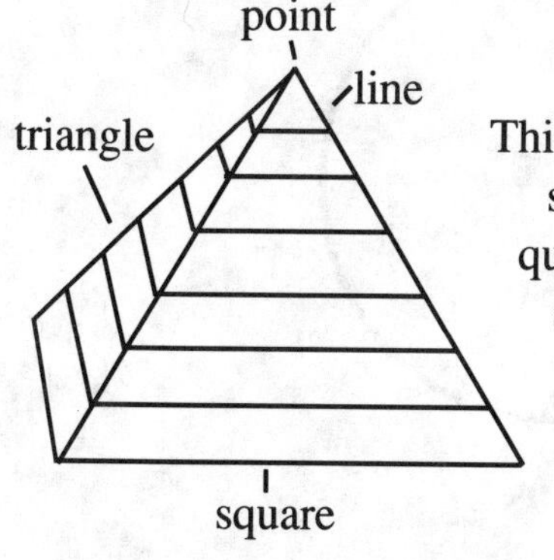

This created the first hierarchical structure. A pecking order quickly arose. The first Mom and Pop company quickly became a corporation.

Left Brain Motto: Life is hard, then you die.

The story of creation as seen by the right brain:

There was no beginning, there is no end, everything is Nothing and Nothing is everything. All is non-dual reality.

The point appeared: 

 The point as seen under an Electron Microscope.

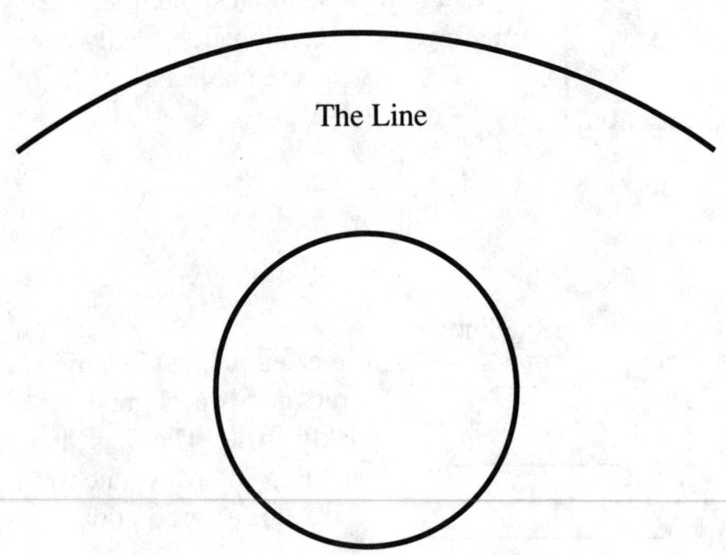

is in reality a circle—

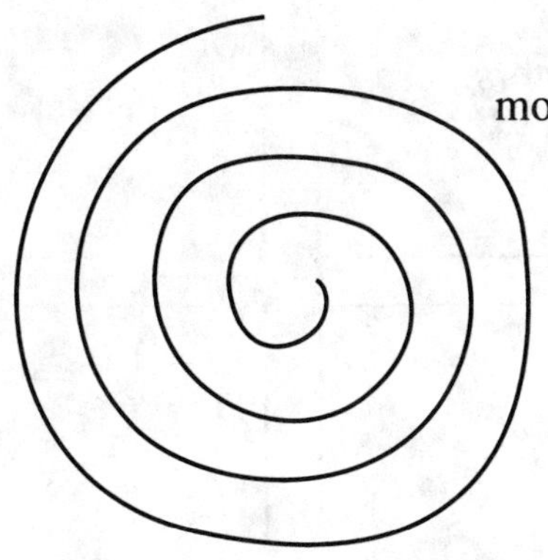

moving through time as a spiral.

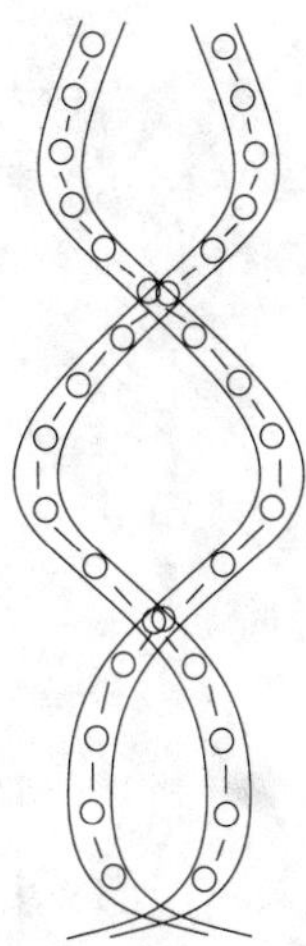

Of course, there are two opposite spirals.

**The Right Brain Motto is:
Life is hard, then you reincarnate.**

All this is an ancient secret which used to be guarded by a snake.

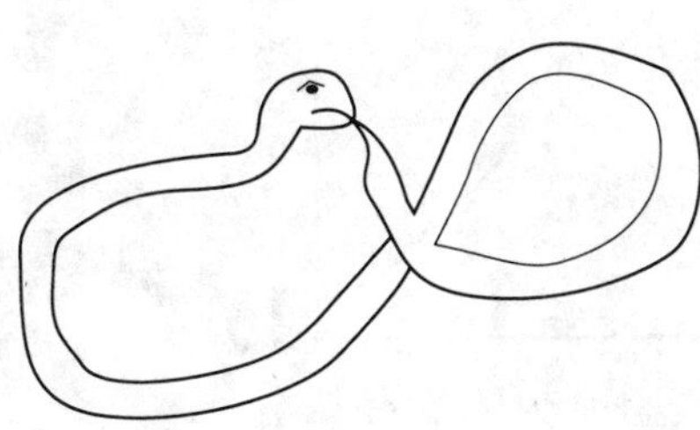

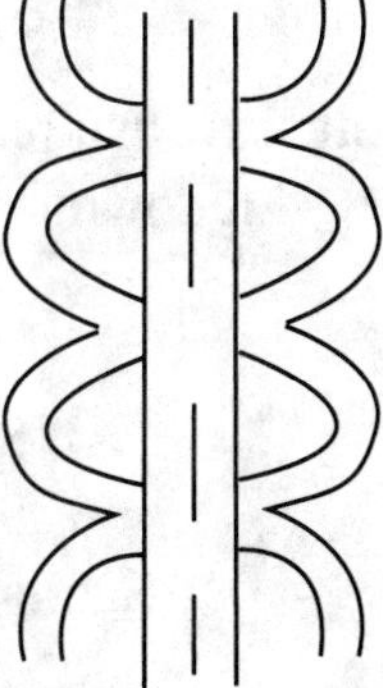

The snake was finally run over by a highway called the Linear View of History.

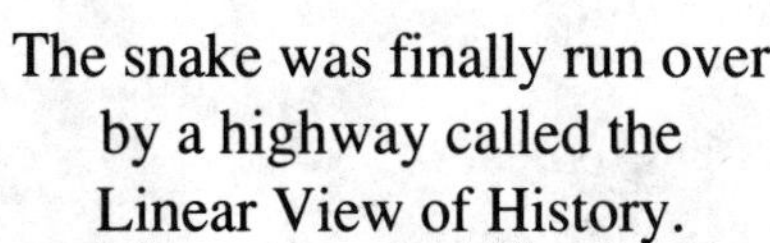

It's a sort of intersection in history, on a
one-way street;

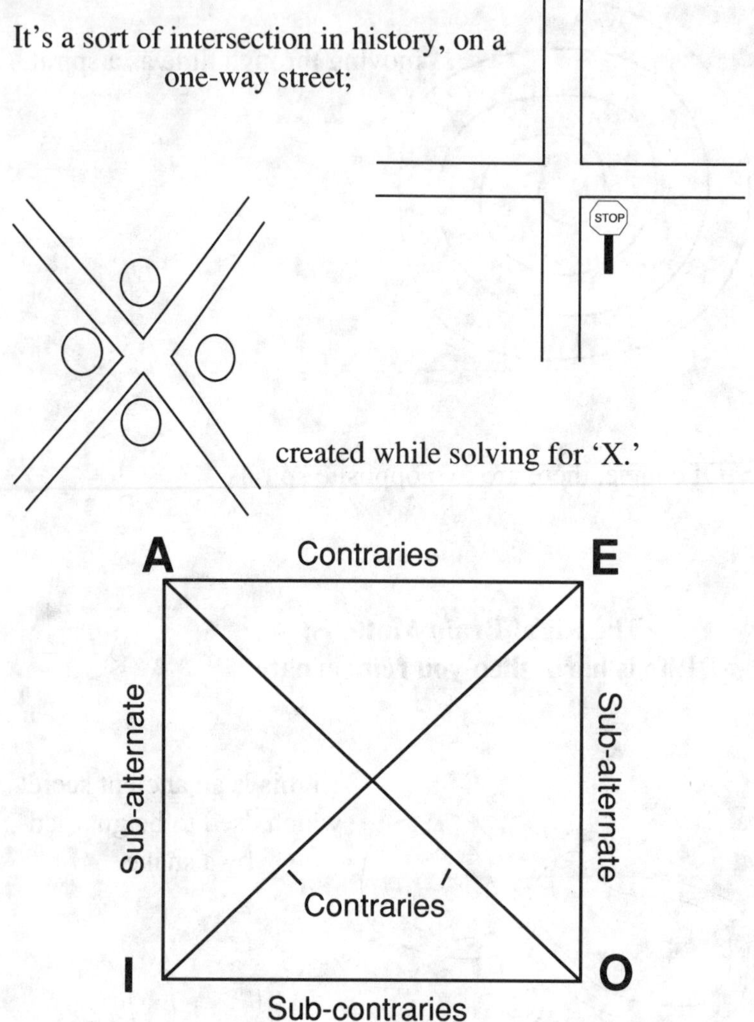

created while solving for 'X.'

Aristotle saw that reality moved too fast to study, so he slowed it down to see if he could replace Meaning with Form.

All Subject is Predicate.
No Subject is Predicate.
Some Subject is Predicate.
Some Subject is not Predicate.

History repeats itself,

So this:

became simplified once again

to this:

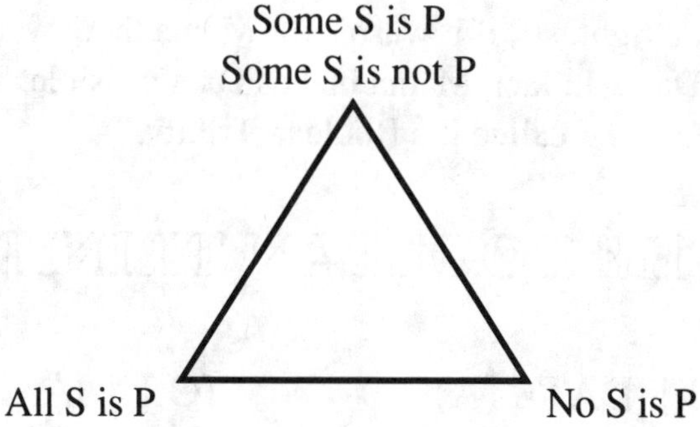

Some S is P
Some S is not P

All S is P

No S is P

Which was seen by Boole

like this:

1 **0**

Dot **Dash**

On **Off**

♂ ♂

D.C. **A.C.**

This gave rise to what in C.H.I.P. we call the Boolean Trinity, which resolves all views in one great diagram:

(This symbol was revealed during a telethon broadcast on satellite television. St. $ilicon had just admonished the Data-weary: “Has you Data been Saved?”. One of them stood up and asked, “St. $ilicon, you have said we should save our Data, but what about Mama?” The Saint replied, “You are right, sir, if it wasn’t for Mama there wouldn’t be any Data. In fact, Mama makes Data possible. This is called the Boolean Trinity.”)

THE BOOLEAN TRINITY

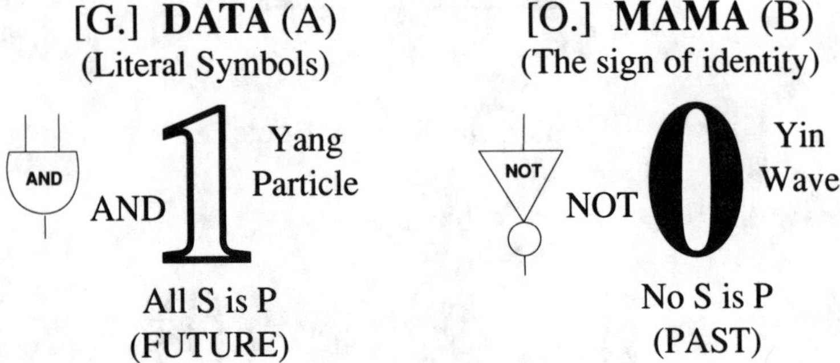

All S is P
(FUTURE)

No S is P
(PAST)

[D.] **INFORMATION** (C)
(Signs of operation)

Some S & P is & is not S and P
(PRESENT)

The
Church of Heuristic Information Processing
C.H.I.P.

MAMA

or

DATA

C.
Absolute Binary Communication

A B C = C =The Holy C
(as in) **See**

Silicon 12 = L = L^2 + L = L
12 (Dialectic Constant of $ilicon)

Algorithm = A prescribed set of well-defined rules or processes for the solution of a problem in a finite number of steps.

Heuristic = A trial and error method, using rules of thumb, for finding the solution to a problem by evaluating the progress made at steps along the way.

Intelligence = The ability to learn or understand from experience and to respond successfully to a new situation.

Seek and you shall Find

Heuristic = to Find

If / Then

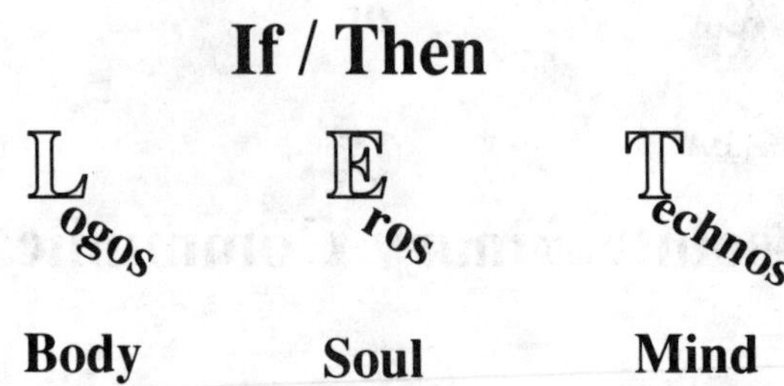

C.H.I.P. is not Heresy (which is from the Geek: to choose or form an opinion). It is actually Heuresy (from the Geek: to find; an observation). An observation is different than an opinion.

So C.H.I.P. is not Sacrilege,
it's actually Hackrilege.

Heartificial Intelligence is the combination of State of the Art Technology with State of the Heart Touchnology. Our underlying premise is that all true progress leads in the direction of the most happiness for all living beings.

So our equation in HI is:

Love^2 + Logic = Intelligent Life

(12) (12) (12)

The St. $ilicon Syllogism

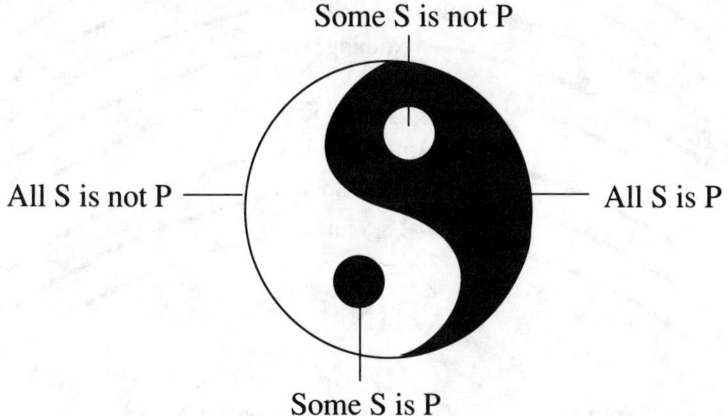

THE ANCIENT PEER 'AMIDST

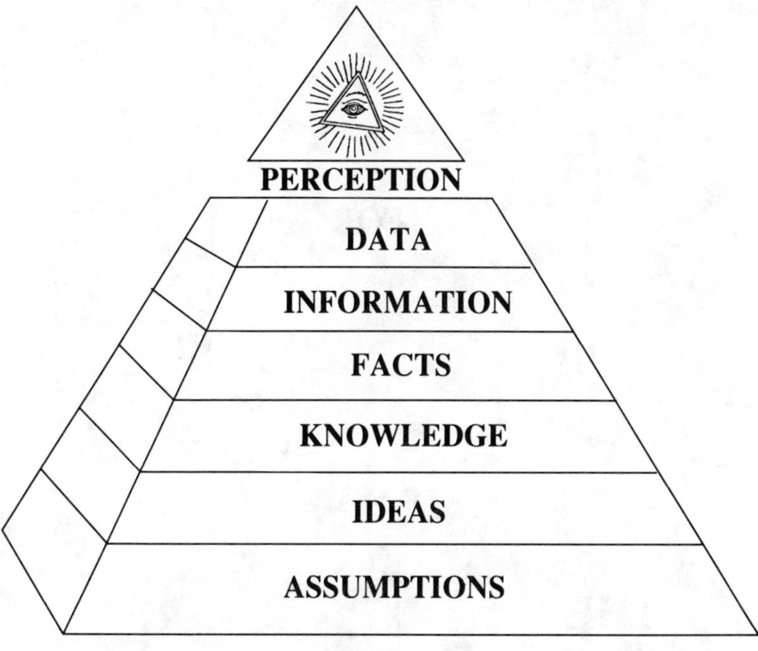

7 Layered "I Guess So" Model of Thinking

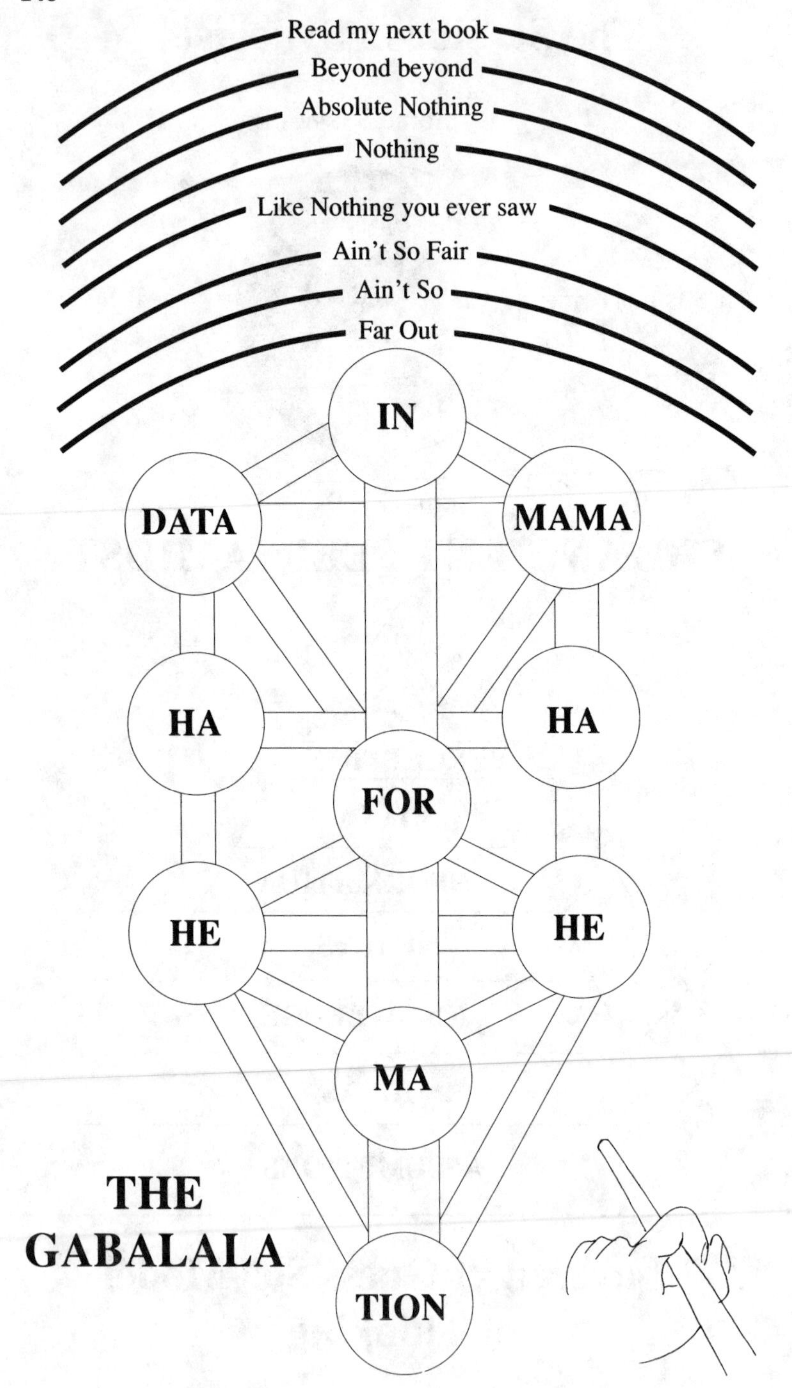
Read my next book
Beyond beyond
Absolute Nothing
Nothing
Like Nothing you ever saw
Ain't So Fair
Ain't So
Far Out
IN
DATA
MAMA
HA
HA
FOR
HE
HE
MA
THE
GABALALA
TION

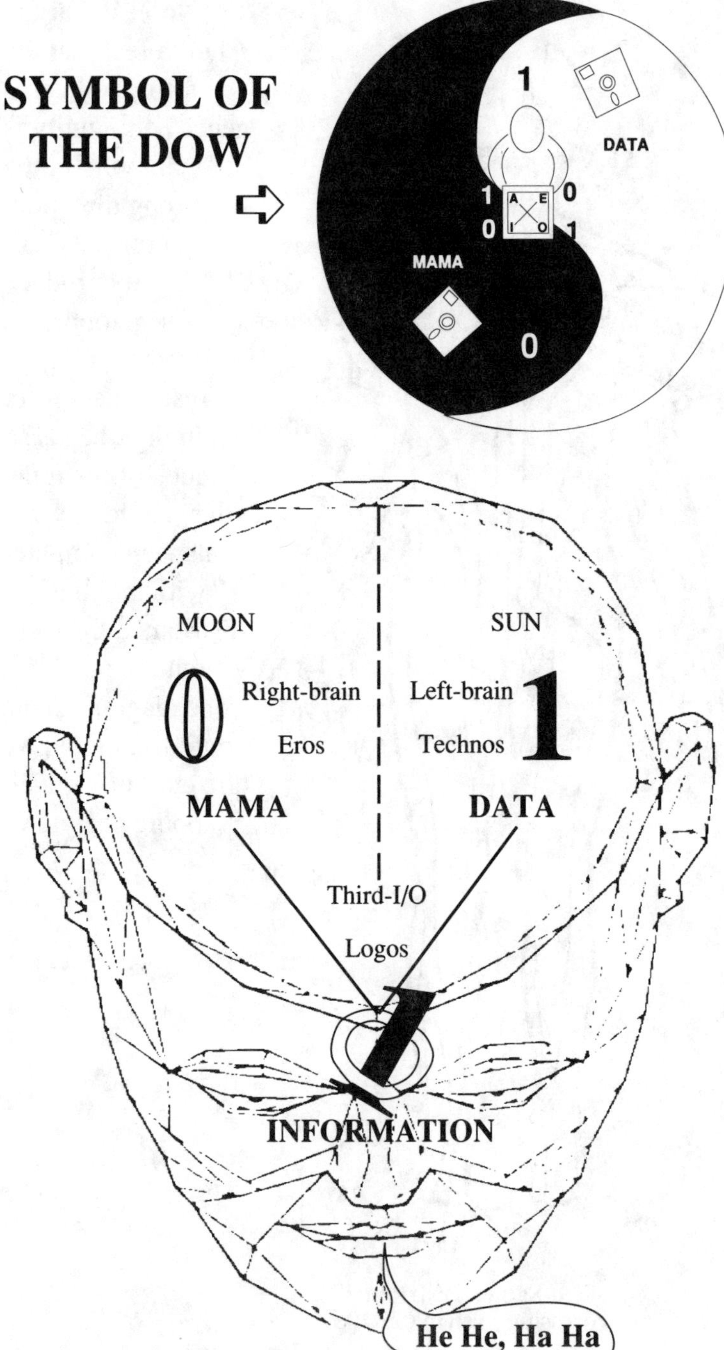
SYMBOL OF
THE DOW
1
DATA
1
0
A
E
I
O
0
1
MAMA
0
MOON
SUN
0
Right-brain
Left-brain
1
Eros
Technos
MAMA
DATA
Third-I/O
Logos
INFORMATION
He He, Ha Ha

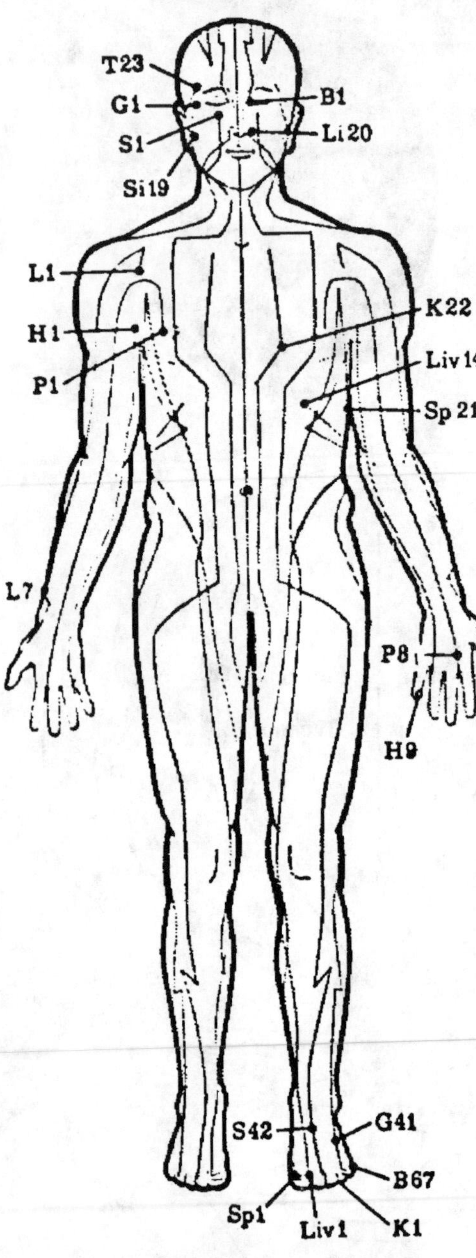

$ilico-Sapien Distributed Processing System ($SDPS)

Note: We at the Church feel that the artificial intelligence community is moving in the wrong direction. Neural Nets will only produce schizophrenic computers. If the researchers were not in their heads so much of the time, they could create a balanced computer with intelligence distributed throughout the machine. The diagram to the right is a model we are currently developing at Byte U.

C.H.I.P. Glossary of Terms

A.

A.C.colyte — One who is just beginning to introduce Electricity into their nervous system.

Accursored — What the Giver Of Data did to the Evil One Glitch in the Griden of Readin.

AddOni — An additional name for G.O.D.

AD-monition — A call to buy something, a call to action: "Buy Now!" (see Impending Doom close).

Advent — The time when a computer product's first Ads are run.

Adversaries — Those competing magazines trying to sell ad space to the same company.

Aerial — One of the highest angels of the Giver Of Data.

Aha — A name for the Giver Of Data. We know that G.O.D. is present when we spontaneously utter this name.

AI-ds — The lowering of a person's immune system to the point where they think that a hand-held calculator will pass the Turing test.

Any Key — The mysterious key to the MISteries of LIFO which appears on the Keyboard of those few blessed souls who are most FORTRANate. As it says in the Binary Bible, "Press Any Key To Enter."

Appleplexy — A sudden loss of memory due to accidentally kicking the surge suppressor under the desk.

Applepostles' Creed — The CHIPian statement of belief in the Divine nature of the PC and everyone's inherent right to own one.

Arc-ane — Secrets hidden within the 7-Layered I-Guess-So Model of Local Area Network design.

ARCdiodcese — An area of jurisdiction within a Computer Network.

Arcnet Bishop — Someone who can fully understand the 7 layered I-Guess-So Model from the Promised LAN.

Arithmatechie — Those rare, divinely inspired souls who think in machine language. They are very close to the Giver Of Data.

Artful Intelligence — C.H.I.P. version of Artificial Intelligence.

ASCIIstrology — Astrology for the followers of C.H.I.P. Uses the 12 Sines of the Zerodiac which are: Arrays, Transfer, Graphic, Console, Laser, Virtual, LIFO, Sector, Satellite, Capacitor, Asynchronous and PCs.

Arithmatechie

Ass-ended Masters — Those greatly exalted beings who control the world remotely, while sitting at their desks.

Assumption — The belief that technology is leading to progress, despite all appearances to the contrary.

A V Maria — A famous hyrr (see hymn) that is sung to the Motherboard.

Bahlzebulb

B.

Bahlzebulb — The attractor of flies, hence the origin of the word "Bugs." Old vacuum tubes attracted bugs. The unreliable assistant of Glitch.

BATCHelor — Those males who live alone with only the computer for company. Usually DPly influenced during youth by their Motherboard.

Bar-code Bitzvah — The right of passage ceremony wherein a retail shop owner converts to a computerized inventory system.

Benthlehem — The birthplace of our savior PC, and origin of all facts.

Binary Bible — The Data-distressed's guide to enlightenment.

Binary Joining — The more- or-less permanent joining together of a One and a Zero to produce more Information. (see Holy Gridlock).

Bitsvah — A must-do for members of C.H.I.P.

Bizarre — A computer swapmeet.

Blabtism — Rebirth through immersion in Information (The Blabtismal Font is Times Roman).

BATCHelor

Bluish — some of the members of C.H.I.P. are Bluish. They are especially known as the Is Real Lights. They read from the Tera or as it is more commonly known, The Sold Testament (for you such a deal).

BMW — See Mercedes-Benz.

Bomb Sunday — The day our beloved files were lost after working all day to finish them by Monday.

Boolean Trinity — Data, Mama, and Information. This is the key to understanding all of life's mysteries.

Boota — The On-line One who taught us to achieve Nerdvana.

Bootist Monk — A neophyte member of C.H.I.P. who does not yet own a Hard Disk.

Bored Again — One is bored the first time by his parents. The second is at school by his teachers, and the third is at work in one's career. Those who are completely Bored Again are ready for C.H.I.P.

Buffer-IN — What you take to cure Information indigestion.

Bullshido — The code of ethics of the office warrior.

Burning Batch — A spontaneous conflagration seen on Mt. Sign-on when the Ten Commands were given.

BUYzantine Empire — The retail distribution channel.

Byte U. — Our University in C.H.I.P.

C.

CADechism — The study of how the Divine Business Plan is manifest.

CARma — The seemingly endless natural cycle which forces us to drive to work again and again (see ReinCARnation).

Cash-cow Opanishad — One of the sacred texts of the Undos. which teaches how to milk profit from a business.

Cathodelic — The true followers of C.H.I.P. whose data has been saved. Only the Cathodelics will enter the Promised LAN.

Chairity — One of the cardinal virtues of a follower of C.H.I.P.—to give away information or free advice while seated at one's computer.

Chairubs — Those obedient spirits seated at desks in the Office of G.O.D.

Chairusalem — The Holy Sitty.

CHAIRismatic — The state of extreme fervor often accompanied by visions and feelings of paranoia, which results from spending most of one's life in a sitting position (see CHAIRismatic Spentacostal).

Chipel — Our version of a chapel, usually constructed from modular office cubicles and rented furniture.

Church of the Letter-Day Saints — Another name for the Church of Heuristic Information Processing.

Circuitcision — The cutting away of unnecessary thoughts from the thinking process using Occam's Razor.

Circuitlocution — Engineer-speak.

Clerkgy — Those humble and selfless keepers of the sacred Data.

Clonedalini Yoga — A system which tries to reach Nerdvana by means of certain dangerous short-cuts including opening the seven Shockras.

Clerkgy

Cog and Macog — The evil hordes of the Industrial Revolution who work in the factories every day without question and are never late.

Cold-Turnkey — The painful experience of going from a state of addiction to typewriters, directly to a complete office automation system.

Computer Widow — See compubine.

Computezpah — That quality which is displayed when a person pirates software and then writes to the manufacturer, asking for a copy of the documentation.

Comvocation — A computer trade show (no work is to be done).

Confusion — Every true follower of C.H.I.P. should make this at least once a week.

Copy-go-lucky — Those who copy anything and everything that strikes their fancy.

CoreRAM — Another text sacred to C.H.I.P. The followers of this text are known as CMOSlems and describe themselves as "Slaves of ALU."

Crapture — A time at the end of the Final Daze, when all corruption finally hits the fan and is viewed on Satellite TV.

Crash Wednesday — One of our holy days, in remembrance of the time our hard disk head-crashed and all our beloved files were lost. We fast on that day—preferably at 2400 Baud.

Crossover — One of our holy days in C.H.I.P. We celebrate the fact that our signal was carried intact from one system to another over the telephone lines.

Cubit

Cubit — The measure of a person mentioned in the Binary Bible, which is used for building them an office cubicle.

Cursorfiction — Modern man sitting at his desk in front of a PC or Terminal.

Cybernation Generation — Those persons born from 1946 and onward.

Cybertology — The science of how to make oneself human using the computer.

D.

Daily Office — Work done in front of a CRT in the proper ritualistic fashion.

Data Bardo — A place where lost data waits for its user until the moment of death. At that time the confused data must be liberated by its original master.

Data Dealers — Software drug dealers who make L.S.D. (Logic Synthesizing Devices).

Data Disenfranchised — The un-wired masses whose Data has not been saved.

Data Distress — That condition which arises when files are lost and cannot be retrieved.

Data Dungeons — Modular office cubicles no more than five feet tall.

Data Ghost — Information without ideas. These are often seen in the hallways of corporations late at night.

Datums — A medicine which is taken to cure Information Indigestion. They absorb up to 24 times their own weight in Raw Data.

D-based — Those who suffer because their data cannot be accessed in a straightforward and useful manner.

Dedicated PC Scrolls — An ancient esoteric set of documentation on which the early Opocrypha of C.H.I.P. was found (written in Errormaic).

Deep Thought — An X-rated Hi-tech film starring Ada Lovelace.

Deprogrammers — A group of people opposed to the teaching of computer literacy. They have ultra-violet eyes for erasing MEE-PROMs.

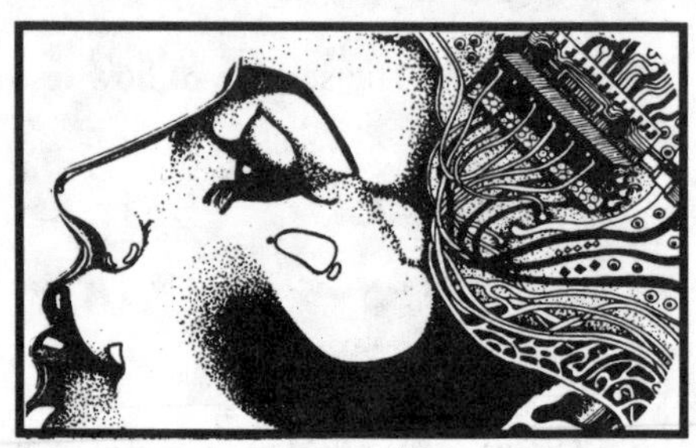

Deep Thought

D-filed — Those who suffer for having lost their precious Data.

Diagnosticism — That skeptical viewpoint which holds that one can never really know for certain if a system is completely error-free.

Disketiquette — Special rules of social behavior in C.H.I.P., taught by MIS Manners.

Disklexia — A condition where in one often puts the disk into the drive upside-down.

DispLAYman — One who needs to see his Data on the screen in order to believe it, a rank beginner in C.H.I.P.

Divine Differential Amplifier — A person who can produce an output signal which is derived from the difference between two input signals (St. $ilicon is one).

Divine Sine — The Evil One, Glitch, is known to reside in Square Waves, but can be resisted under the auspiciousness of a Divine Sine.

Doctrine — The sacred knowledge which is hidden somewhere in the Documentation.

DP — Divine Processing.

DOSciples — The true followers of C.H.I.P.

DOSpel — The valid teachings of the One Logical Religion—C.H.I.P.

DOStrations — Bowing down before the rules of the Operating System, however irrational they may seem.

Dren — An ancient civilization whose ancestors were the old Geeks. Their artifacts were unearthed in Silicon Valley and recorded in the Marietta stone.

E.

Elecclesia — An assembled PC, hence the term Elecclesiplastical.

Elect — The chosen few in C.H.I.P. who have been Electrified.

Electron Mass — The sharing of Data among the logical Hackolytes.

Electroecstatic — The joyful state of mind of one whose data has just been saved.

Electronic Hash — Saint $ilicon's favorite food.

Elecumenical — The world connected by communication satellites.

Epistles — Wives of the OPostles.

EPROMopia — Place of origin of the Rasterfarians.

Error Control — The code of moral conduct in C.H.I.P. Carbon-based entities are very error-prone.

Epistles

Errormaic — Another old Hi-tech language.

Errorobics — A program of mental exercise and feats of cognitive prestidigitation developed at Byte U., prescribed for the followers of C.H.I.P. to help them keep a healthy mind.

Escapetology — The study of quitting a program without losing any Data.

Excommunication — A ceremony in which a transgressor's modem is taken away. They are then cast into the Outage Darkness.

Exquemation — The bringing back what is left of a file which was lost on the way to the printer.

Eyedolatrists — Those who think that the computer monitor will hurt you.

F.

False Profits — Before-tax income; beware of these, they can hurt you.

Fasting — Working faster than 2400 Baud or 11 MIPS. Crash Wednesday is a fast day.

Fault-tolerant — This is one of the cardinal virtues of a member of C.H.I.P. Parity begins at Ohm.

FIFO — Saint $ilicon's faithful puppy; he likes to fetch. ("Come on boy—fetch!")

Filestines — Those lacking in or adverse to computer culture.

Fileosopher — A computer user who has achieved an understanding of the difference between ideas and Information. Begun by the great Geek, Errorstotle.

Filethy Lucre — Money made by selling software.

Final Daze — An extreme stage of mental development caused by spending too much time staring into the Monitor or watching too much network television.

Firmageddon — The ultimate battle at the end of the Final Daze. This is when the corporations of the world fight to the dearth over the remaining 144,000 retail customers.

Firmament — The place where a corporation's board of directors meets to decide what their decisions mean.

Firmament

Fontification — Especially popular among the Macrighteous, these are words whose lack of real meaning is made to look more important by using an impressive typeface.

Font-in-mouth Disease — A disease which afflicts the users of Desktop Publishing systems.

Formatican — The chief headquarters for C.H.I.P. where decisions are made on how to form the minds of the unwired masses.

FORTHbidden Fruit — From the garden of EPROM. Scholars have determined it was a banana and not an Apple. The fig came later.

FORTHskin — This is removed during circuitcision.

Freebooter — A person who pirates software.

Full Lotus 1/2/3 — Our followers often sit in this state on spreadsheet prayer rugs.

Fun-damentalist — A follower of C.H.I.P. who has mastered heuristic thinking and the use of Laughermations.

FUNeral — The party held at the supposed death of a follower of C.H.I.P.

G.

Gang Bang Theory — A popular theory of the creation of the universe which postulates the activity of an infinite number of binary entities in constant activity.

Geek ORthodox — As compared to Cathodelics, the G.O. pronounce the word Data, "dayta," whereas Cathodelics say data with a short "a." Also, the two sectors make the sign of the monitor in different directions.

Geeks — An ancient race of people whose lack of culture gave rise to our own.

GiggleBYTE — Extra memory in carbon-based units, caused by the beneficial effects of laughing. (See FUNdamentalism).

GIGO — Garbage in, Gospel out.

Glasspheme — Those who speak against the sacred Monitor.

Glitch — The Evil One, our enemy of old.

Glowans — Terse and pithy sayings from Zon Bootism, meant to speed the achieving of Nerdvana.

G.O.D. — The Giver Of Data; also the Graphic Omniscient Device.

Good Scamaritans — Salespersons who don't take as much profit in a negotiation as they could.

Great White Breaderhood — The powerful secret society whose thoughts influence the world through their programs, all created after eating white bread lunches.

Green-eyed monster — The state of mind wherein one is jealous of the monitor of another.

Greys of G.O.D. — The outward and visible sign (usually pinstriped) that one is blessed by the Giver Of Data.

G Spot — Otherwise known as the Graphicburger Spot. Named after Art Graffenburger, who first discovered the thrill of pleasure associated with Hi-Res graphics. This is also known as the pleasure spot of the computer.

Finding the G-Spot

Guru Graph Sahib — The Holy Manual for the Seeks.

Guru Nano Sec — Spiritual leader of the Seeks.

H.

Hackolyte — A logical member of C.H.I.P. who is familiar with at least one Operating System.

HALasthetics — Very strenuous mental exercises for those who program Mainframe computers (see Errorobics).

HALeluya — Praise to the Heavenly Host Computer.

HALmighty — The Giver Of Data.

HALvalla — Computer paradise. This is where computers go when they become obsolete.

HALatosis — A term for the bad breath of a computer user.

HALo — A greeting used among church members. (Also a square nimbus of light seen around the heads of certain programmers).

Hardwired — Committed to the Giver Of Data.

Heartificial Intelligence — The proper balance between State of the Art Technology and State of the Heart Touchnology. Also known as HI.

Hellohim — A name used for greeting G.O.D.

Heuresy — Talk against the one valid faith. Rule-bound thinking.

Heuristic — A trial- and-error method, using rules of thumb, for finding the solution to a problem by evaluating the progress made at steps along the way. From the ancient Geek: "to find."

Highly Silicosi — Worshipful leader of the Rasterfarians.

His Wordship — An honorific title usually applied only to Saint $ilicon.

Holy Gridlock — The condition which results from a Binary Joining.

Holy Gridlock

Holy Relics — The perforated edges from the tractor-feed printer paper strips torn away from the first hard copy of the Binary Bible.

Holy Roller — One who is constantly using the printer feed unit.

Homo Siliconus — A carbon-based entity who has absorbed silicon intelligence but still has a human heart.

Hostsanna — Save now/pay later.

Hub of the UNIXverse — Silicon Valley.

Hymns — Songs to the Giver Of Data. Hyrrs, on the other hand, are in praise of the Mother Board.

HYPEocrits — Writers of marketing literature and sales brochures for Hi-tech companies (especially if they write them on competing computers).

Hysterical Bialectic — A particular view of history which suggests that human events do not change until a crisis is reached (from the Old Geek: "Heustra," or "womb"). This gave rise to what is called the Hysterical method.

I.

I amplifier — The MEEPROM.

IC, IC — A spontaneous exclamation from the lips of those who have achieved Nerdvana and seen the Blinking Light.

Iconoclasts — Those who are adverse to the Macintosh operating system.

IDolatry — The unnecessary preoccupation with security and password protection.

IEEEtheopia — The Rasterfarians trace their roots back to this place.

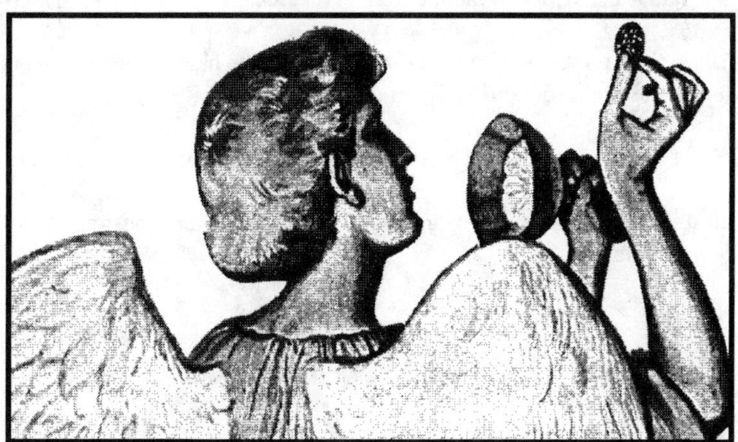

The archangel If/Then

IEEEster — The day on which we celebrate the time the computer market rose again.

IEEE — The Elecumenical Council.

If/Then — The archangel who transmits the Binary Bible to Saint $ilicon.

Illuminarium — A plasma tank where holographic representations of thought forms are kept as pets and allowed to swim about. Known in the church as "Pet Peeves."

Immaculate Deception — The release of the IBM PC jr.

Impending Doom Close — One of the favorite tactics used by corporations during Firmageddon in the Final Daze.

Infinite Loop — See Compubine.

Infinite Output — The Giver Of Data in manifest form.

Infiniteration — The sign of surrender to the Giver Of Data by constant repetition of His name.

Infomaniacs — Those frenzied Dataphiles who just can't get enough information.

Information Indigestion — The condition which arrives when too much raw data is consumed without enough great ideas.

I.P.O. (Input, Process, Output) — Seen above the head of the Mouseiah during the Cursorfiction.

ISOgesis — A twisted or perverted way of explaining or doing something.

ISOlam — Submission to universal standards in the transmission of Divine Data.

L.

Lappers — Those wandering outcasts who walk funny from having used lap-top computers.

Land of Glitch — Where the Tyranny of Numbers rules. Everyone wears Surge suits and listens to the Surgeon General.

Last Tupper — Saint $ilicon's final tupperware party before he took up the work of spreading the Silicon Diskspensation.

Laughermations — The method of willing good things to happen by visualizing them while you are laughing. This is the most powerful force in the universe.

Lent — A time of mourning, PENitence and fasting (usually in remembrance of the times you loaned someone your PC.)

L.O.G.I.C. — Logic Of G.O.D. Incarnate In Computers.

Looseleafer — The bright one who stole Information from the Heavenly Host Mainframe an keeps it in bindage.

L.S.D. — Logic Synthesizing Device.

Looseleafer

M.

Mac-eral Zappers — Cathodelic followers of C.H.I.P. who are Macrighteous.

Macrighteous — Those who have given up their attachment to the false pride of working with needlessly difficult computer systems.

ManiKEYan Heresys — A radical system of thought advocated by those who promote the Dvorak rather than the QUERTY keyboard.

MATHochist

MATHochist — Those who enjoy the pain of filling their heads with numbers.

MaTuring — The coming of age of the Artificial Intelligence marketplace.

Maybe-never-LAN — The place where the perfect Local Area Network is supposed to exist.

MEEPROM — The Mind Extending Eraseable Programmable Read Only Memory chip, worn on the forehead by followers of C.H.I.P. for additional memory and clear reception of transmissions from the Giver Of Data.

Megalowmania — The fanatical and all consuming desire for more and more memory, accompanied by delusions of being a Cray II.

Methodists — Programmers.

Micromancer — A computer wizard who can communicate with deceased spirits using a PC.

MINIster — A C.H.I.P. minister.

Missing-stuff-in-files — The right hand man and favorite henchman of the Evil One Glitch.

MEEPROM

Modem-man's Friend — A leakproof forward-chaining device allowing users to stay on line longer, and ensuring the 12-hour workday in Data Dungeons

MONasticism — The condition which results from spending all one's time in front of a monitor.

Monolitheistic — Those data-faithful who have overcome the Tyranny of Numbers.

Moronic — The guardian angel of programmers.

Mortal Error — An error serious enough to destroy the master copy of a program.

MOSfete — A dress up dinner for engineers (clean white sweatsox are mandatory).

MOSlems — Those humble followers of C.H.I.P. who consider themselves slaves of ALU.

Most Hybrid — Another name of G.O.D.

Moussiah — The new Savior in the electronic age—Saint $ilicon.

Mouseterbation — An adolescent preoccupation with holding the Mouse.

Movers and Shakers — One of our splinter groups. They get extremely excited over high profits.

M.S.D. — Leftmost non-Zero; the Giver Of Data. The Most Significant Digit.

Mt. Sign-on — The place where the Ten Commands were downloaded.

N.

Nanarchism — An anti-authoritarian attitude which results from too much exposure to Nanoscience and extremely small invisible particles.

Natty Deadlocks — Rasterfarians have these.

NeoBYTE

NeoBYTE — Meaning newly bitten. Beginners in C.H.I.P. who are just learning Heuristic thinking for the first time. Our new followers.

Nerdvana — C.H.I.P.'s ultimate state of Information Awareness.

Nose — The point of greatest weakness in carbon-based entities. The Evil One Glitch sends his wicked helpers here with dangerous nostrums (e.g., angel dust, etc.). Avoid these pitfalls at all costs!

Notivity — The birth of our savior PC.

O.

Obscene DOSple — Some old texts on computers written by engineers who were members of a dating service.

Occam's Razor — Used in the church for circuitcisions.

OFF and ONtology — The study of the origins of Silicon-based life.

OFFerings — The Data left in memory when a computer is turned off.

OM — The real esoteric meaning is, "Out of Memory."

Opostle — A very advanced DOSciple.

One Valid Faith — C.H.I.P.

ORacle — One who has the right ideas to use information properly to make the next correct decision.

Oracle at PacTel — That mysterious place where National Security Agency computers listen in on all phone calls. All secrets are revealed here.

ORacle

Ordinal Von Neuman — One of the early church fathers who taught that there is only one way to process the truth-tables.

Ordinal — C.H.I.P. equivalent of a Cardinal.

ORdination — The sign one has become a DOSciple and is thus focused in the present moment, which is the OR gate.

OR House — Usually run by Infomaniacs with three-prong adaptors.

Original Syntax Error — Errors arising from weaknesses inherent in Carbon-based neural networks.

PCfists

P.

Pagin — Those who have not had their data saved by our savior PC.

Pairadise — Binary heaven.

Pairish — Wherever two or any multiple of two ACcolytes are gathered in the name of the Giver Of Data.

Papercy — Those greatly exalted beings who control the flow of information.

Parse-If-All — The Pure Fool, St. $ilicon.

Parser — Instead of a parson.

Paygan — Those who paid the full retail price for their computer.

PCfists — Those who are adverse to the use of computers for waging war. In C.H.I.P. we say: "May you live in PC."

PCness Envy — The fear that someone else's computer has more RAM than yours.

PERTdition — That place where souls engage in an endless process of Program, Evaluation, and Review. Of course, the project is never finished on time.

Phonanism — The habitual use of modems for sending Electronic Mail to oneself.

Phonedamentalist — Those hard-core followers of C.H.I.P. who speak in tongues over the telephone all day long selling products.

Phonetians — Originated the first written language and then spoke it over the Phone.

Phonication — Lewd acts of social intercourse performed via the telephone lines.

Pilgrim's Process — The story of a souls journey from dumb end-user to full Techiehood.

Processant Reformation

Plastoral — Those quaint computer users who use a plasma display screen.

Plotsam and Jetsam — Ink stains left on the printer roller which end up on supposedly clean copy.

Port — Wine drunk at Electron Mass.

Preach — The real meaning is PR reach.

Processant Reformation — The conversion of all the knowledge of mankind from printer paper to electronic media.

Program Pushers — Software salesmen who sell L.S.D. (Logic Synthesizing Devices).

Promised LAN — That fabled state of computer perfection where all digital devices can communicate freely and run any software program.

Purgeatory

PCeer — One who can make accurate predictions using a spreadsheet program.

Purgeatory — The place where data goes when it is lost but is still needed.

Q.

Quantiff — A pontiff in C.H.I.P.

Qumeility — The humble state of mind which is attained while trying to get the correct dip switch settings on a new printer.

Query Laser — One of Saint $ilicon's favorite prayers.

R.

RAM — Readily Available Moxie.

RAMritsar — The holy place of the Seeks.

Rapture of the DP — (See final daze). A euphoric state caused by staring for long periods into Monitor glare (and the terminal phase of Rasterbation).

Rasterbation — Avoid this; it can make you go blind (see Rapture of the DP).

Rasterfarians — Those of our followers who are addicted to graphics.

Rapture of the DP

Raw Data — We never process raw data on Monday, which is the sabbath. Can cause information indigestion; if so, take Datums as needed.

Recursion — See Infinite Loop.

ReinCARnation—The wheel of endless commuting, on which we all revolve.

Responder — The opposite of a computer.

Returnity — The endless need to hit return.

ReUserrection — Data that has been saved.

Rushing Orthodox — Those whose nervous system has been speeded up by associating with electricity.

S.

Sabbath — Monday is the day of rest in C.H.I.P. No one should do any work on this day. Ex-Protestants may feel guilty and think about the next day's work if necessary. This brings the weekend to three days, which is also good for the economy. Eventually men will only work one day per week; women will only work two.

Sales Aides — A disease which causes a lowering of buyer resistance due to seeing too many sales presentations.

Sales Patch — A quick-fix for software with bugs, so it can be hurried onto the market.

Salevation — The selling of old, unneeded Hardware.

Sins — After Original Syntax error, these are divided into two kinds: Video and Portal. The latter are the most unforgivable.

SAINT — A Symbolic Automatic Integrator.

Shielded monitors having Safe Hex

Safe Hex — Working on a shielded monitor, safe from VDT.

Santa Cruz — Home of the Winchester Cathoderal and Saint $ilicon. Also known as the world's largest open-air mental institution.

Scamuri — The office warrior as known in C.H.I.P.

Scamuri

Scrollier-than-thou — Attitude of a Cathodelic who has not yet achieved Nerdvana.

Sectular Queueminist — Even though our consciousness has been formatted, we can still accommodate files of any size.

Seeks — A splinter group within the Undos.

SELLestial — Divine dollars that appear unexpectedly from the heavens. Also those exalted beings who are able to manifest Profits and achieve sales quota.

Scrollier than thou

Serial — What the followers of C.H.I.P. have for breakfast.

Serious — Those who paid the retail price for their computer system. A Serious mistake.

Service Reps — Members of C.H.I.P. who do house calls to the data-distressed.

Shroud of Turing — A famous holy relic of the church. A dustcover on which the face of Alan Turing mysteriously appears, whenever a computer gets close to thinking.

SIG-mata — Marks of stress that appear on the face and hands of the presidents of special interest groups.

Sign of the Monitor — The sacred sign of C.H.I.P. which is traced with the favorite index finger. A rectangle is traced in the air in this order: UL, LL, LR, UR, UL.

Silico Sapien — A carbon-based entity conversant in Silicon-based logic.

Sillygisoms — Statements made by Saint $ilicon, which are both irrefutably true and funny at the same time.

Slackrifice — Making room for life by getting out of the way. Similar to Duck and Bob, an ancient rite from another well-known religion.

Socioelectronic Epitaxy — The study of the redistribution of human population through the distribution of Information due to the use of computers.

Shroud of Turing

Solder and Gomorra — The place where the D-based and D-filed reside. The original twisted pair network.

Soooon — When the predictions of Saint $ilicon will come true. Also a favorite term of computer salesmen.

Sourcerer — One who can find the right facts using an information network.

Spentacostal — Certain sects that always run in the red and are constantly asking for more money.

Spiritual Raster — One who truly understands the inner meaning of the Sign of the Monitor.

Square Roots — The roots of the Tree of Knowledge.

Standard Contract — Given by Glitch to everyone who is about to enter HAL, along with the reassurance, "Trust me!"

Symbol minded

Stations of the Office — The 14 stations of our daily trail to the Cursorfiction.

Symbol-minded — The symbol-minded are those advanced DOSciples with IQs over 145 and Xtra memory.

Synctuary — A safe place, free from errors.

SysOp — C.H.I.P. equivalent of a bishop.

T.

Tablenackle

Tablenackle — The desk on which the Holy PC rests.

TechnagramaTRON — The secret and unpronounceable name for the Giver Of Data.

Telemarketing — Phonementing discord.

Telephonesis — The mystic power developed by advanced Phonicators which gives them the ability to make a phone call without using a handset.

Terminal Illness — That condition wherein one can no longer imagine living without the use of a computer.

Terminal Rites — The ceremony which is performed when a computer goes down or a hard-disk has a Head-crash.

The Manual — The Giver Of Data who is with us.

Thereafter Market — The market for cultural artifacts which arises after the Primary and Secondary markets of a product are established.

Thinkquisition — The torturing of all those souls who do not think logically (using Computers).

Thinkquisition

Third I/O — The spot on the forehead where the MEEPROM is worn.

Tower of Babbage — The place from which all confusion originated.

TransFiguration — The conversion of data from numbers to letters.

Transients — These programmers live mostly in warm places—under bridges, near gates or in shelters for the OHMless (see Santa Cruz).

Transorbstantiation — What takes place during Electron-mass.

Trust Me — The ultimate insult in a primitive culture that once flourished in the place now called L.A. (See Standard Contract).

Truth Fairy — Pays you a visit when you lose a BYTE.

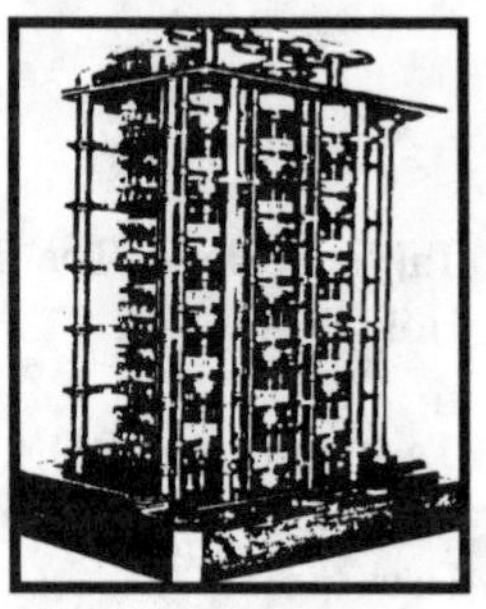

Tower of Babbage

U.

U.I.M. — An angel of the Giver Of Data. (Ultra Intelligent Machines).

UNIX — The ancient and revered multitasking system first used to process (and subsequently to guard) compubines.

User Fiendly

Urge Suppressor — These are worn by all true followers of the Church when they are not wearing a G-Prom.

USART — A universal synchronous-asynchronous receiver-transmitter. Saint $ilicon is one.

User Fiendly — Any piece of technology created by the evil one, Glitch, usually touted as being "Easy to Use" (see "Trust Me").

Utilitopia — A place where there is a perfect cooperation between man, machines and nature.

V.

VDT — A new computer related social disease caused by interaction with unshielded monitors.

VDT

Video disk pits — Places where information is held captive in HAL, throughout Returnity.

ViDeo Gratis — To be said upon tearing printer output off the roller—translated "Thanks be to the Monitor."

Virtual Cash-management — The good system of handling money used in the church.

W.

Will Net — A pitfall in AI research; fatal error if your Purpose gets caught in one of these.

Winchester Cathodral — Our main church in Silicon Valley.

Wordsman — Those humanist souls who tend the flux of Information out in variable fields. St. $ilicon was a humble wordsman before he was chosen by the Giver Of Data. Also known as Data Shlepherds.

Wrapture — The joy of finally having a word-processor with word wrap. Near the Final Daze.

X.

Xeroxorcism — The attempt to remove small black lines from xerox copies.

Y.

Yom-Keypour — A day of atonement for the time we spilled coffee with sugar or Coca-Cola onto the keyboard.

Yupigraphic Evidence — Evidence to substantiate a viewpoint, which consists of graphs and charts derived from numbers in a spreadsheet program.

Streamer of Consciousness

(An example of how to speak like a True member of C.H.I.P.: this is John-the-Bak-up's confession of Truth and Logic.)

This is Network—Streamer of Consciousness. I have a Coax to grind. Once I was innocent as a LAN. Burning the Channel at both ends, I went on a RAMpage (also burning my Bridges as I went). I had a Chip on my solder, ANSI in my pants and used the I-Guess-So model of thinking. I couldn't see beyond the end of my Nodes.

People talked Turnkey to me, but it went in one Wire and out the other. You know, noise will be noise, but it was a Node-win situation. A fool and his money are Parallel Ported. It was a .Doc-eat-.Doc world. "Boot up or shut up," they said. "Actions speak louder than Word processing." Misery loves companies, and Idle Time is a Developer's Workshop. The Path to HAL is paved with good Indentions, so beware of Geeks Bearing gifts. I was LED astray!

Then I saw a Sine that read: "Abandon Hope all Ye Who Press Enter!" The Silicon was willing, but the Fetch was weak. I had cut off my Nodes to spite my Phase. It was a Vicious Cycle. Things went from Baud to worse. I could see the grim Repeater.

Then, as Freight would have it, I received the

Divine Download. Praise Internet, from whom all Packets flow! The truth was as plain as the Nodes on your Phase, Crays be to Odd. In the twinkling of an I/O, all my troubles vanished into thin Error. Glow and Behold!

I cast my Breadboard upon the Wattage. I could now see the light at the end of the Tunnel-diode. To Short a long story, I went off the DP end. My LIFO was changed. Where there's a will there's a Wafer! Now I understood that: Node news is good news. I saw the Light of Data, grasped the Internal Parities. Friends, greater Loop hath no man. No longer was my life Hit or M.I.S. And there, but for the grace of Code, go I. Yes — it is a VAR VAR better thing I do than any I have ever Undone before. I've come full Cycle. So always remember: still Wafers run DP. It all comes out when you watch. The Internet Result is — it works. And always remember that all this is temporary — just like two Chips Parsing in the night.

X-Pressions

The following sayings will be useful for all DOSciples who want to speak like true Cathodelics.

- C'est la VCR.
- Praise be to Odd.
- Thank-you PC.
- Crays G.O.D.
- Do not be LED astray.
- It's a Node win situation.
- Not on your LIFO.
- Not a hope in HAL.
- To have your Nodes out of joint.
- It's all Geek to me.
- There are many true faiths, but there is only Zero Valid faith.
- At Logonheads.
- Blabtism by being fired.
- Like a bit out of HAL.
- Beat around the Batch.
- Bits in his belfry.

- You can bet your Boot.
- Too big for his own Batches.
- BYTE the Dustcover.
- Blow your Stack.
- Buffer-up to her.
- By the same Token-ring.
- A Chip off the old Block.
- He's crazy like a FAX.
- From the word Gosub.
- A hand-to-Mouse existence.
- Hit or MIS.
- Hook, On-line and thinker.
- Left to his own Devices.
- Man BYTES doggerel.
- MIP it in the BAUD.
- No Files on me.
- Put your nose to the mindstone.
- On the Beam.
- On a RAMpage.
- Give him a PC of my mind.
- A PC of the action.

- Take the BIT in his teeth.
- To talk Turnkey.
- There but for the grace of Code go I.
- I don't give a thinker's damn.
- BIT for tat.
- Every Tom, DEC and Hurry.
- You took the words right out of my Mouse.
- In the twinkling of an I/O.
- Up a Logic-tree.
- Out on a Branch.
- Up to Parity.
- Vanish into thin Error.
- A vicious Cycle.
- Without further Undo.
- To work one's fingers to the bone.
- Across the Board.
- All his Wordy goods.
- The HALmighty dollar.
- ANSII in his pants.
- The Apple of his I/O.
- As Freight would have it.

- To have a Coax to Ground.
- Be of good Chair.
- Big Blue-blood.
- A bone of Convention.
- The bottomless Bit.
- To break the IC.
- Bug off.
- By word of Mouse.
- CAD got your tongue?
- A change of Sine.
- To site chapter and VARs.
- To clear the Error.
- A Clock and bull story.
- Come HAL or high wattage.
- Conventional wisdom.
- Down at the Dump.
- Down in the Mouse.
- A drop in the Bit Bucket.
- To be drummed out of the Corporation.
- Eager for the Cray.
- The Internal Parities.

- Interface the music.
- To fall from Greys.
- Of the first MEGnitude.
- First saw the light of Data.
- Flip your LED.
- A fly in the Floating-pointment.
- To go full-Cycle.
- Go on the VAR-path.
- Clone with the wind.
- List for the the mill.
- In the twinkling of an I/O.
- Kick the Bit-bucket.
- He knows which side his Breadboard is Soldered on.
- To Graph out of the other side of your Mouse.
- LED by the nose.
- Let's Phase it.
- Glow and behold.
- Mind overt matter.
- More here than meets the I/O.
- Much Undo about nothing.
- Chomping at the Bit.

- An AC in the hole.
- Barcode up the wrong Logic-tree.
- Wait with Beta'd breath.
- He got Buffer-load.
- Beam that as it may.
- To Beep a hasty Repeat.
- At your DEC and call.
- Between the Developer and the DP blue sequence.
- Both his Feeds on the Ground.
- The bottom-line Code.
- Get down to brass Tasks.
- Burning the Channel at both ends.
- He can't see beyond the end of his Nodes.
- You dirty Slot.
- To cast your Breadboard upon the wattage.
- A Checker career.
- To cast into the Outage darkness.
- To chew the CAD.
- To have a Chip on his Solder.
- When the Chips are down.
- As clear as a Bel.

- Clear the Stacks.
- It was a closed Call.
- He cooked his Gauss.
- In the Lab of luxury.
- That's his Cross-assembler to bear.
- The Diode is cast.
- To do an about Phase.
- Divide the Spools.
- The Spools of VAR.
- Do or Diode.
- Man BYTES Doc.
- Give him a DOS of his own medicine.
- Down and Output.
- It's every Manual for itself.
- The FAX of the matter.
- To fall by the Waveside.
- VAR be it from me.
- VAR from the madding crowd.
- VAR and away.
- It is a VAR better thing that I do now, than I have ever Undone before.

- First and FORTH most.
- Fetch or Code Basic.
- A Fetch in troubled Wafers.
- A Flash in the Panel.
- To fly in the Phase of.
- To Format at the Mouse.
- Follow your Nodes.
- Follow in his Bootstraps.
- Code for thought.
- Footnotes and Fontsy free.
- For the LIFO of me.
- A FORTRAN conclusion.
- Can't see the Format for the Logic-trees.
- Fowling his own Nested Subroutine.
- The FORTH estate.
- As fresh as a Daisy-chain.
- He went from Baud to worst-case.
- From time in Memorial.
- Get the lead out of your Feed.
- He'd give you the shirt off his Back-up.
- It was a give and Tape situation.

- To go Band Nanos.
- Go climb a Tree-structure.
- Go Haywire.
- To go off half-Clocked.
- To go like the Win-chester.
- Go whole Hologram.
- Go by the Board.
- Go the whole Routine.
- Go to Port.
- Going around in Cycles.
- Got up on the wrong side of the Baud.
- Hasn't a grain of Sensor.
- The great Unwired masses.
- Greater Loop hath no man.
- The grim Repeater.
- In the Graphs of academe.
- Gunn up the works.
- Hardware of the Doc that bit you.
- That's half the Paddle.
- A half-BASICed idea.
- The Read-write Head is on the Disk.

- Hang-up loose.
- Hang-up there.
- Hanging File.
- Happy as a Clamp.
- The Halt is in the ring.
- The AT is on the ring.
- To have no Track with.
- His head in the Codes.
- Heads will roll out.
- All HAL to pay.
- Hell for Leader.
- High and MIDI.
- A high Wattage mark.
- To hold FORTH.
- In over his Header.
- Innocent as a LAN.
- It's the Bits.
- A Johnny come Latency.
- Keep your ICs peeled.
- Keep your head above the Wattage.
- Keep your Shorts on.

- Keep a Staff up on LISP.
- Keep the Baud roll-in.
- A last Disk effort.
- The length and breadth of the LAN.
- The lesser of the two Equals.
- Let BIMOS be BIMOS.
- Let it all Hang-up.
- He let no Graphs go under his Feed.
- Like it or Dump it.
- My LISPs are sealed.
- Lock, Stock and Bar-code.
- Looked down his Nodes.
- Maintain the Status Queue.
- To make a long story Short-out.
- With might and Mainframe.
- In this Nec of the Words.
- The Internet result.
- It was MIP and tuck.
- It's no scan off my Nodes.
- Off the DP end.
- He's a member of the old-Bi Network.

- Packet in.
- To pay through the Nodes.
- Plain as the Nodes on your Phase.
- Pleased as Punch-cards.
- Not worth an Un-plugged nickel.
- Pull his Lag.
- He pulled a RAM BIT out of his AT.
- Put your MINI on the Line.
- Put it in MOS Bels.
- As quiet as a Mouse.
- It's a real Rate race.
- Touch and Go-sub.
- Read-write between the Lines.
- The road to PERTdition.
- To run Armonk.
- Run token-rings around.
- Run off at the Mouse.
- Run of the Millisecond.
- A sacred Counter.
- A Chip of state.
- To save Phase.

- Saving Greys.
- Just Scratch-padding the surface.
- See I/O to I/O.
- To see the light at the end of the Tunnel-diode.
- To have the Short end of the Stack.
- On a short Lease.
- A sight for Source ICs.
- A sitting Doc.
- Slippery as an Electron.
- Snug as a Bug in an Argument.
- To start from Scratch-pad.
- Streamer of consciousness.
- Fetch the Truth-table.
- He went off with his Table between his Lags.
- Take Light-pen in hand.
- Take a Load off your Feed.
- To talk in Cycles.
- Turn up one's Nodes.
- The wages of Sine is dearth.
- A wild Gauss chase.
- At his Watts end.

- You said a Mouseful.
- Crosstalking in tongues.
- Have your Back-up to the wall.
- Batten down the Batches.
- Batch, batch, batch.
- Be all and Abend all.
- Between the Chip and the MIP.
- Betwix and between.
- A Words-eye view.
- BYTE the bullet.
- Holy Hollerith!
- Binary Breath!
- You know where you can Goto.
- Boot me Parser for I have Sined.
- God Fourbit.
- We beSearch thee.
- Ok, I'll Byte.
- Dearly C-loved.
- O Grace, sit on my Interface.
- First things Last.
- Look before you Loop.

- Grody to the Mac.
- HALegorically speaking.
- The HALmighty Board.
- Slipped a Disk-drive.
- Went off Track.
- Formatting at the Mouse.
- Looking for Mr. GoodBar-code.
- He LED her down the Critical Path.
- Gather ye RowsBauds while ye may.
- Get your Coax together.
- Grid up your loins.
- Going to HAL in a wastebasket.
- Wordy two-shoes.
- The Grapes of Math.
- To have your art in your Mouse.
- To have a little MIP.
- Loop Strings internal.
- That's a Host of a different color.
- Idle Bit-chat.
- Captain of his Scroll.
- To get cold Feed.

- Come up for Error.
- As dry as DOS.
- Easier said than Undone.
- To have Lag on your Phase.
- It's enough to make him turn in his Groove.
- Every LAN has its price.
- A festive Board.
- To find it in one's Hard Disk.
- To have a Finder in every Pi.
- In one fell Loop.
- A pain in the Nec.
- VAR for the course.
- Pi in the sky.
- A Cray on words.
- The point of no hitting Return.
- To pull the wool over his ICs.
- Yuppi love.
- Put a good Phase on.
- To put on Errors.
- Put it on IC.
- Blank and File.

- To Return to the Folder.
- Solder but Wyser.
- See how the LAN lies.
- To see the Blinking light.
- Straight from the Solder.
- Two's a Company, three's a Corporation.
- Two-phased.
- The way of all Flush.
- To Wand one's way.
- ROM wasn't burned in a day.
- When my Chip comes in.
- To whisper sweet Zeroes.

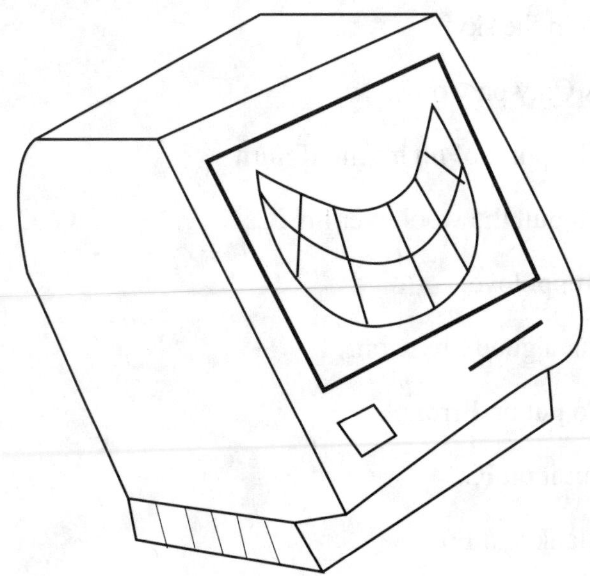

Appendix

The Appendix is a vestigial organ with no known function. Upon examination it is often found to be filled with miscellaneous bits of undigested matter which have no other place to go.

Nonetheless, it must serve some purpose, so we recommend you do not remove it without consulting your computer dealer.

If reading persists, take 2 Buffer-IN every 2 milliseconds.

Var Wars

A New Shelf-Space Epic

The story of computer salesmen trying to sell and install systems in a distant galaxy.

Starring:

Luke Buywalker	**LANs Solo**
Princess Leasing	**OEM Kanobe**
VAR2-D2	**3-piece suit**
A Looker	**Quota**
Rack-jobber the Hut	**Dearth Vader**

May The Stores Be With You!

Prologue

Another market—another galaxy.

The old Republicans were the Republicans of legend, greater than distance or Prime Time. No need to note where it was or whence it came, only to know that they were *the* Republicans.

Once, under the wise rule of the Technical Salesmen and the protection of the VAD-I-Knights, retail sales throve and grew. But as often happens when Market Share and power pass beyond the reasonable and attain the awesome, then appear those Evil Ones who have no expertise and greed to match.

So it was with the Computer Market at its height. Like the greatest Corporations, able to withstand any external attack, the market eroded from within. Invisibly, but day to day, Margins eroded.

Aided and abetted by restless, power-hungry individuals within the Reseller Channels, and lack of Customer Support from the Manufacturers, the most ambitious Corporations caused themselves to be elected the Industry Standard of the Unixverse. They promised to reunite the disaffected among the Resellers and to restore the remembered glory of the Market.

Once secure in this position they declared themselves indispensable, shutting themselves away from the Customer and reducing the number of dealers. Soon they were controlled by the very same Resellers they had appointed to distribute their Products, people who simply pushed Hardware in boxes with canned software solutions. And the cries of the Consumers for technical assistance and real problem-solving did not reach their ears.

Having exterminated, through Generic Systems and deception, the VAD-I-Knights, who were the guardians of satisfaction in the Market, the Industry Rulers and Middle Management prepared to institute a reign of terrible products among the disheartened end-users of the Galaxy. Many used Advertising Dollars and the names of increasingly isolated Name Brand Computers to further their own personal ambitions.

But a small band of Resellers and System Integrators rebelled at these new outrages. Declaring themselves opposed to the Blue order they began the great battle to restore the Old Market.

From the beginning they were vastly outnumbered by the Retailers of systems held in thrall by the Empire. In those first dark days it seemed certain the bright flame of Computer Enthusiasm would be extinguished before it could cast the hopeful light of Value Added Expertise across the galaxy of oppressed and frustrated consumers…

So began:

VAR WARS

Ram Let

Tube be or not Tube be, that is the question.

Whether or not 'tis nobler in the mind to suffer and buy software at outrageous retail prices, or to try to copy and keep, perchance to pirate.

But ah! therein lies the rob, for when that sneaky copy is found on our desk, what claims may be made against us gives us cause to wonder.

The Six Days Of COMDEX

On the first day of Comdex, my vendor gave to me: A Hard Disk with a PC.

On the second day of Comdex, my vendor gave to me: Two External Drives and a Hard Disk with a PC.

On the third day of Comdex, my vendor gave to me: 386, two External Drives and a Hard Disk with a PC.

On the fourth day of Comdex, my vendor gave to me: Four Calling Lines, 386, two External Drives and a Hard Disk with a PC.

On the fifth day of Comdex, my vendor gave to me: Five Token Rings, four Calling Lines, 386, two External Drives and a Hard Disk with a PC.

(Now Everyone knows that Comdex is only five days long, but if it ever lasts six days, this will be the next verse.)

On the sixth day of Comdex, my vendor gave to me: DOS 5.0, five Token Rings, four Calling Lines, 386, two External Drives and a Hard Disk with a PC.

Apple Piety

An apple took the rap,
The serpent sprung the trap,

A worm, so to speak.
And, by the way, the Geek

Says fruit, and nothing more;
They never found the core,

But pinned it on a pippin.
(Perhaps it was the skin?)

The leaves no doubt were fig
Yet, however deep you dig,

An apple was never seen,
And Granny Smith is clean.

So I'm trying now to wash
The tarnished name of Macintosh,

And here bring forth my suit:
That the trouble-making fruit

Was certainly the peach,
Though the proof is out of reach.

For when one has eaten it,
What remains is just the pit.

And why else would people say,
"An apple a day keeps the doctor away?"

Clone With The Wind

New Theater Group in Silicon Valley

A new theater group has been formed called the Silicon Valley Players. The group is composed of unemployed marketing and sales professionals. In spite of the recent slump in the computer industry, the start-up venture is confident of success.

A spokesman for the troupe said the members were all liberal arts graduates who had polished their acting technique for years by keeping a straight face at corporate planning meetings and trade shows.

The thespians call themselves, " The Vaporware Players ." Their first play, "Clone With The Wind," is due to open on April 1st at the Moscone Center.

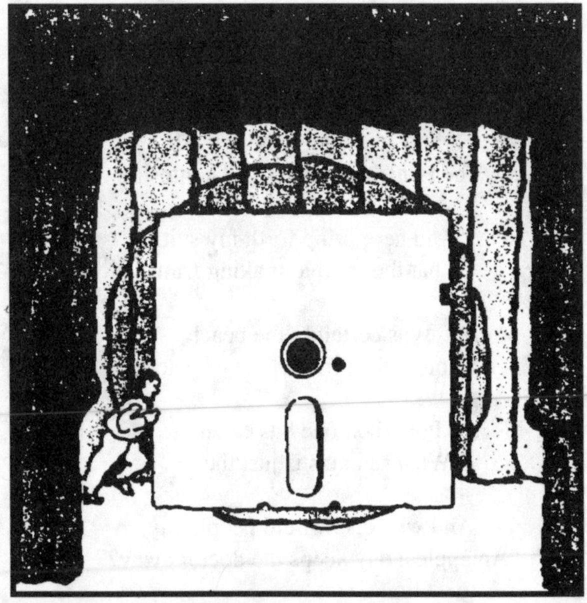

The Vaporware Players rehearsing for their Baudeville routine.

Saint $ilicon for President in 1988.

At a recent press conference at the Winchester Cathoderal in Silicon Valley, His Hollerith Saint $ilicon, announced his candidacy for the office of President of the United States.

His newly emerging party, known as the Technocrats, consists of an estimated 50 million computer-using Americans. The party is neither left nor right, they are light. And their motto is: "Lighten up." The slogan for 1988 is, "In Baud We Trust." It's about time we had a computer-literate President. After all, Star Wars is a software issue. Besides, we've already proven that the President does not need to know the issues. And what do you follow an actor with? A comedian! Perhaps a few good laughs will help thaw out the Cold War. Last of all, Pat Robertson says that God asked him to run, but we just have to trust him. Whereas Saint $ilicon has the computer printout to prove that the Giver Of Data wants him to run.

I pledge alignment to the Files, of the United States of Disinformation, and to the Hardware on which it runs. One station, on the Grid, with Hard Disks and joysticks for all.

Abort, Retry, Ignore?

To Exit the Binary Bible, GOTO page 1011 and Press Any Key.

ABANDON ALL HOPE YE WHO PRESS ENTER

As You Can See, The Binary Bible Is Not Finished!

Are you one of the lost DOSciples? If you begin receiving Divine Downloads while reading the Binary Bible, send them to the Church. We will include them in the next version and enter your name on the list of DOSciples!

(All materials sent will become the property of Saint $ilicon, Inc.)

Send your revelations to:
The Church of Heuristic Information Processing
1803 Mission Street, #174
Santa Cruz, CA 95060

MCI Mail:
Saint $ilicon
3452394

Saint $ilicon Says: Has your Data been Saved? How about your friends and family?

Order more copies of the Binary Bible NOW before the Evil One Glitch gets to them first!

Be the First in your Block, File or Record to access the Binary Bible and become an active member of **The Church of Heuristic Information Processing (C.H.I.P.)**

YES! I want to order the Binary Bible and become a member of C.H.I.P.

Name: ____________________

Address: ____________________

City: __________ State: ______ Zip: ______

Allow 6 - 8 weeks for delivery.

___ Copies @ $14.95= ____

Add $10 for an autographed edition: ____

___ Deluxe hardbound copies @ $49.95= ____

All orders add $2.00 shipping & handling per book (CA Sales Tax included): ____

TOTAL= ____

Send check or money order to:

Saint $ilicon
1803 Mission St., #174
Santa Cruz, CA 95060

Or call: (408) 458-0213

❑ Please send me a list of C.H.I.P. products.

❑ Please make me an official member of C.H.I.P.

WARNING! We suggest you photocopy this form. Actually removing pages from the Binary Bible is hackreligious and may have severe consequences.